T0220236

Pro Ember Data

Getting Ember Data to Work with Your API

David Tang

Apress®

Pro Ember Data

David Tang
Playa Vista, CA, USA

ISBN-13 (pbk): 978-1-4842-6560-4   ISBN-13 (electronic): 978-1-4842-6561-1
https://doi.org/10.1007/978-1-4842-6561-1

Copyright © 2021 by David Tang

Managing Director, Apress Media LLC: Welmoed Spahr
Acquisitions Editor: Louise Corrigan
Development Editor: James Markham
Coordinating Editor: Nancy Chen

Cover designed by eStudioCalamar

Cover image designed by Freepik (www.freepik.com)

Distributed to the book trade worldwide by Springer Science+Business Media New York, 1 New York Plaza, New York, NY 10004. Phone 1-800-SPRINGER, fax (201) 348-4505, e-mail orders-ny@springer-sbm.com, or visit www.springeronline.com. Apress Media, LLC is a California LLC and the sole member (owner) is Springer Science + Business Media Finance Inc (SSBM Finance Inc). SSBM Finance Inc is a **Delaware** corporation.

For information on translations, please e-mail booktranslations@springernature.com; for reprint, paperback, or audio rights, please e-mail bookpermissions@springernature.com.

Apress titles may be purchased in bulk for academic, corporate, or promotional use. eBook versions and licenses are also available for most titles. For more information, reference our Print and eBook Bulk Sales web page at http://www.apress.com/bulk-sales.

Any source code or other supplementary material referenced by the author in this book is available to readers on GitHub via the book's product page, located at www.apress.com/9781484265604. For more detailed information, please visit http://www.apress.com/source-code.

Printed on acid-free paper

This book is dedicated to my wife, Elaine Lin, who went to bed without me on many occasions because I wanted to learn, play with, or write about Ember. This book would not exist without your love and support and I will always be grateful.

Table of Contents

About the Author

David Tang is a Software Engineer from Los Angeles with over 10 years of working experience in web development. His software career has led him to work with companies of all sizes and use many different technologies on both the backend and frontend for building web applications. Ultimately, he found his passion on the frontend in building applications with rich user experiences. He has worked with several JavaScript frameworks, but was drawn to Ember because of the community's values in convention over configuration, developer testing, and the commitment to providing an upgrade path for new major releases. He values the framework's opinionated way of working with APIs and managing data in a client-side JavaScript application with its companion library Ember Data. Since David was introduced to Ember, he has spent a lot of time blogging, teaching, and building applications with Ember and Ember Data. David is also an adjunct faculty member at the University of Southern California, teaching web development courses.

About the Technical Reviewer

Alexander Chinedu Nnakwue has a
background in Mechanical Engineering from
the University of Ibadan, Nigeria, and has been
a frontend developer for over 3 years working
on both web and mobile technologies. He also
has experience as a technical author, writer,
and reviewer. He enjoys programming for the
Web, and occasionally, you can also find him
playing soccer. He was born in Benin City and
is currently based in Lagos, Nigeria.

Acknowledgments

I would like to thank the Ember team and everyone who has contributed to Ember for making such a productive framework for building modern web applications that is a joy to work with. I would especially like to thank Chris Thoburn for sharing his knowledge on Ember Data with me.

Introduction

Why I Wrote This Book?

Let me tell you my story. I was drawn to Ember because of all the great things you hear about it, like convention over configuration, an out-of-the-box test harness, and stability without stagnation. I also really liked that Ember had an opinionated way to work with APIs and handle data in a JavaScript application with its companion library Ember Data. Ember Data has features like models, model relationships, and identity mapping, which addressed challenges I had previously experienced when building client-side applications. I followed along through various tutorials using Ember Data where the API was already set up. Then I decided to use Ember on a real project where I wasn't in control of the API. The API's request and response payloads didn't match the format that Ember Data expected. For example, I had a payload structure like the following, which doesn't work with Ember Data out of the box:

```
{
  "data": [
    { "id": 1, "firstName": "Yehuda" },
    { "id": 2, "firstName": "Tom" }
  ]
}
```

I did a little research and started seeing terminology like adapters, serializers, transforms, embedded records, and snapshots; the large Ember Data API documentation; and various forum threads suggesting different solutions that I couldn't get to work. I quickly felt overwhelmed and had a hard time proceeding forward. I definitely considered using the good old `$.ajax` wrapped in a service instead, but I knew I'd be missing out on a lot of great features in Ember Data, my application would be less conventional, and I'd probably be reinventing the wheel. I made the decision to start digging into Ember Data and learning everything I could about it so that I could leverage the power of this amazing library. I'm glad I made that choice.

So why did I write this book? I want to help you learn how to adapt Ember Data to your API so that you don't get frustrated and give up on Ember or Ember Data. Once you understand how Ember Data works, I bet you'll come to appreciate it and enjoy using it like I do.

Is This Book for Me?

This book is for anyone interested in learning more about Ember Data. Maybe you've been using `$.ajax` and would like to start using Ember Data. Maybe you've used Ember Data with an API that follows the default conventions, and you are looking to learn more about what's going on under the hood. Maybe you want to write your own adapter and serializer to work with a particular backend. This book is for anyone with an interest in learning more about Ember Data. If you haven't used Ember Data before, Chapter 1 – Ember Data Overview provides a short introduction, but I recommend reading the section on Ember Data in the Ember Guides[1] to get acquainted.

---

[1]`https://guides.emberjs.com/`

Tools

In order to use the sample applications for this book, please install the following tools:

- Git (`https://git-scm.com/`).

- Node.js (with npm). Any modern version should do. I tested with v12.*, which is the LTS version at the time of this writing (`https://nodejs.org/`).

- Google Chrome.

- Ember Inspector Google Chrome Extension (`https://github.com/emberjs/ember-inspector`).

- Ember CLI (`https://ember-cli.com/`).

Conventions

When I use "JSON:API", I am referring to the JSON:API specification.[2]

API Documentation

Throughout the book, I will refer to various APIs in Ember Data like classes, functions, and mixins. If at any point you aren't sure where to import them from, check out the Ember Data API documentation[3] or the Ember Data Packages RFC.[4]

---

[2]`https://jsonapi.org/`

[3]`https://api.emberjs.com/ember-data`

[4]`https://github.com/emberjs/rfcs/blob/master/text/0395-ember-data-packages.md`

Errata

I have done my best to ensure this book doesn't have any typos and errors. If you do find mistakes however, please file an issue on the book's GitHub repository (`https://github.com/Apress/pro-ember-data`).

Get in Touch

Do you have questions on any of the material in this book? Do you need help getting your API to work with Ember Data? Feel free to reach out to me on Twitter at @iamdtang or send me an email at david@thejsguycom.

CHAPTER 1

Ember Data Overview

This chapter is meant to provide an architectural overview and basic summary of Ember Data. If you haven't used Ember Data before, I recommend reading the section on Ember Data in the Ember Guides[1] to get acquainted. This chapter will provide a foundation of how all the pieces in Ember Data fit together so that you can start customizing it to fit your API.

Architectural Overview

Ember Data's architecture can be diagrammed as follows.

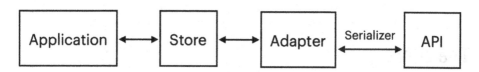

On the left is the application, which interacts with the store. By default, routes and controllers have access to the store, for example:

```
import Route from '@ember/routing/route';

export default class ContactsRoute extends Route {
  model() {
    return this.store.findAll('contact');
  }
}
```

---

[1]https://guides.emberjs.com/

© David Tang 2021
D. Tang, *Pro Ember Data*, https://doi.org/10.1007/978-1-4842-6561-1_1

The store can also be injected into other parts of an application like components:

```
import Component from '@glimmer/component';
import { tracked } from '@glimmer/tracking';
import { inject as service } from '@ember/service';

export default class ContactsListComponent extends Component {
  @service store;

  @tracked contacts;

  constructor() {
    super(...arguments);

    this.store.findAll('contact').then((contacts) => {
      this.contacts = contacts;
    });
  }
}
```

The Store

The store is an instance of the Store class, and it is a service that acts as a data access layer and cache for the records (instances of models) in an application. It is responsible for instantiating models on the client and saving the data via an API. The store can also request data from an API and turn that data into rich client-side models which are referred to as records. These records are then cached for subsequent retrieval.

The store also implements an identity map to prevent multiple references of the same record existing in an application. For example, let's say we make two requests. The first request is for a list of contacts and this list contains a contact with an id of 1. A second request happens somewhere else in the application also for the contact with an id of 1.

This means there are two contact objects with an id of 1 in memory. Manually keeping these duplicate contact objects in sync often results in a poor data architecture that isn't very scalable and reusable. Through identity mapping, the store will keep track of a single contact record with an id of 1. If multiple AJAX requests return the contact with an id of 1, such as GET /contacts and GET /contacts/1, the data will be mapped to a single contact record in the store. Through identity mapping, the store will preserve object identity and return the same records, regardless of how many times you ask for it.

The Adapter

The store delegates the specifics of how to work with an API to an adapter. This is the adapter design pattern in use. Think of the adapter pattern like handling electrical outlets when you travel abroad. If you have a three-pronged electrical plug, it won't fit in a two-pronged wall outlet. Instead, you need to use a travel adapter to convert the existing three-pronged plug configuration to conform to the socket of the country you are visiting. Same idea here, but instead of having an adapter to fit the electrical outlet, you have an adapter to fit your API. Your backend could be an HTTP or WebSocket protocol-based API or even browser storage technologies like Local Storage or IndexedDB. By isolating the specifics of where the data comes from in an adapter from the rest of an application, if the way the application communicates with the backend changes in the future, only the adapter will need to change instead of across the application.

The Serializer

Between the adapter and the API is the serializer. The serializer has two jobs. First, it is used to format data sent to the server, also known as *serialization*. Second, the serializer is used to format data received from the server, known as *normalization*. As we'll see later in this book, Ember Data ships with three different serializers, which can be extended to fit any API.

Now that we have a good idea of the core pieces behind Ember Data, let's go through an example.

Model Attributes and Transforms

To start working with Ember Data, we first need to think about the underlying data in an application and represent them as models. For example, a cat application might have models cat, home, and owner. We can use Ember CLI to generate a cat model class:

```
ember generate model cat
```

This will generate the following model class:

app/models/cat.js

```
import Model from '@ember-data/model';

export default class CatModel extends Model {}
```

Next, we can define the schema of our model via attributes and specify their types using transforms. Transforms allow us to transform properties from the server before they are set as attributes on a record or sent back to the server. Here is an example of the cat model using the four built-in transforms – string, number, boolean, and date:

app/models/cat.js

```
import Model, { attr } from '@ember-data/model';

export default class CatModel extends Model {
  @attr('string') name;
  @attr('number') age;
  @attr('boolean') adopted;
  @attr('date') birthday;
}
```

The built-in transforms are listed in Table 1-1.

Table 1-1. *Built-in Transforms*

Transform Name	Usage
String	attr('string')
Number	attr('number')
Boolean	attr('boolean')
Date	attr('date')

When a model is created, the attributes are coerced to the types specified in the corresponding attr() decorator call. For example, let's say a cat resource came in from the server looking like the following:

```
{
  "id": 1,
  "name": "Frisky",
```

```
    "age": "10",
    "adopted": "true",
    "birthday": "2005-11-05T13:15:30Z",
    "color": "white"
}
```

On the cat record, the name attribute would be set as a string, the age attribute would be coerced to the number 10, the adopted attribute would be coerced to a boolean value of true, and the birthday attribute would be coerced to a Date object. Lastly, because the color attribute was not specified on the model class, it wouldn't get set on the cat record.

Behind the scenes, each of these attr() decorator calls maps to a specific transform class that extends from Transform. If we don't pass anything to attr(), the value will be passed through as is. This can be useful as we'll see in Chapter 8 – Working with Nested Data and Embedded Records.

The built-in transforms are self-explanatory for the most part. The string transform will coerce the value to a string using the native String constructor function. The number transform will coerce the value to a number using the native Number constructor function. If the attribute is not a number, null is returned. The boolean transform not only transforms boolean values, but the strings "true", "t", or "1" in any casing and the number 1 will all coerce to true, and anything else will coerce to false. The date transform will construct a Date object using the native Date constructor function. When a date attribute is serialized, such as when saving a record, the date will be converted to the ISO 8601 format via Date.prototype.toISOString()[2] (YYYY-MM-DDTHH:mm:ss.sssZ).

/

---

[2]https://developer.mozilla.org/en-US/docs/Web/JavaScript/Reference/Global_Objects/Date/toISOString

The API

Now before we continue any further, let's create a JSON:API-compliant API in Node.js with Express that returns hard-coded data. If you aren't familiar with JSON:API, don't worry. We'll be going over that in more detail in Chapter 3 – API Response Formats and Serializers, but if you want to get a head start, check out the JSON:API specification[3] for more information.

Create an api folder with a server.js file:

```
mkdir api
cd api
touch server.js
```

Place the following in server.js:

```
const express = require('express');
const cors = require('cors');

const app = express();

app.use(cors());

app.get('/api/v1/cats', (request, response) => {
  response.json({
    data: [
      {
        type: 'cats',
        id: 1,
        attributes: {
          name: 'Frisky',
          age: 10,
          adopted: true,
          birthday: '2005-11-05T13:15:30Z'
```

---

[3]https://jsonapi.org/

```
        },
        relationships: {
          home: {
            data: { type: 'homes', id: 1 }
          }
        }
      }
    ]
  });
});

app.get('/api/v1/homes/:id', (request, response) => {
  response.json({
    data: {
      type: 'homes',
      id: request.params.id,
      attributes: {
        street: '123 Purrfect Avenue'
      }
    }
  });
});

app.listen(8000, () => {
  console.log('Listening on port 8000');
});
```

Next, let's install the dependencies and run the API:

```
npm install
node server.js
```

If you visit http://localhost:8000/api/v1/cats, you should see a list of cats in JSON.

Using the Store

Now that we have an API running and we've set up our `cat` model, let's start interacting with the store to access data from the API. As stated before, the store is automatically injected into routes. Let's say we have a route for the path /cats:

app/routes/cats.js

```
import Route from '@ember/routing/route';

export default class CatsRoute extends Route {
  model() {
    return this.store.findAll('cat');
  }
}
```

We are using the route's `model` hook to fetch a collection of `cat` resources from our server using the `findAll()` method on the store. This is just one of the methods available on the store, but other common methods include those listed in Table 1-2.

Table 1-2. *Commonly used Store methods*

Store Method	Description
findRecord()	Finds a single record for a given type and ID and returns a promise
peekRecord()	Finds a record in the store synchronously for a given type and ID
peekAll()	Returns all records for a given type in the store
createRecord()	Creates a new instance of a model and puts it in the store

If we run our application and navigate to /cats, we'll notice an error in the console saying that http://localhost:4200/cats could not be found. This is happening because we haven't told Ember Data what the host of our API is. Let's do that by creating an adapter.

Adapters

Ember Data allows us to create an adapter that can be used across our application. This is called an application adapter and can be generated with the following command:

```
ember generate adapter application
```

Alternatively, we can create adapters for specific models:

```
ember generate adapter cat
```

If a model-specific adapter exists, Ember Data will use that instead of the application adapter when working with that model. Otherwise, the application adapter will be used. In this case, we don't need the flexibility of a model-specific adapter, so let's just create an application adapter with the properties host and namespace:

app/adapters/application.js

```
import JSONAPIAdapter from '@ember-data/adapter/json-api';

export default class ApplicationAdapter extends JSONAPIAdapter
{
  host = 'http://localhost:8000';
  namespace = 'api/v1';
}
```

With this change, Ember Data is now hitting our API successfully! I'll leave it to you to render the cat records.

Ember Data uses JSON:API by default for both the adapter and serializer. This is why our application works even without having created a serializer. We'll look at how to create and extend serializers in future chapters.

We're almost done with the basics. We just need to tackle relationships.

Relationships

Models can have relationships with other models. Let's look at a very common relationship, one-to-many.

A cat, if fortunate, belongs to a home. Let's say we want to get the home record from the cat record. We can specify this relationship using belongsTo():

app/models/cat.js

```
import Model, { belongsTo } from '@ember-data/model';

export default class CatModel extends Model {
  // ...
  @belongsTo('home') home;
}
```

Let's say we have a home record, and from the home record we want to access all of the cats for that home. This is the other side of the one-to-many relationship. We can specify this relationship using hasMany() because a home can have one or more cats:

app/models/home.js

```
import Model, { hasMany } from '@ember-data/model';

export default class HomeModel extends Model {
  @hasMany('cat') cats;
}
```

11

Ember Data allows us to define relationships on models both synchronously and asynchronously. By default, model relationships are asynchronous. When an asynchronous relationship is accessed, if the related records aren't already in the store, Ember Data will trigger a fetch and return a promise that resolves with the related record. If that record is already in the store, a promise will be returned that resolves with the related record.

Go ahead and render the home's street address for the cat and see what happens. If you do, you'll notice that a GET request is made to the `/api/v1/homes/:id` endpoint that we defined in `server.js` earlier.

As previously mentioned, a relationship can also be declared as synchronous. When a synchronous relationship is accessed and the related record is already in the store, the record will be returned. If that record isn't in the store, an error will be thrown. To see this in action, change the home relationship on the `cat` model to be synchronous:

app/models/cat.js

```
import Model, { belongsTo } from '@ember-data/model';

export default class CatModel extends Model {
  // ...
  @belongsTo('home', { async: false }) home;
}
```

Next, try and render `cat.home.street` and you will get the following error:

Error   You looked up the 'home' relationship on a 'cat' with id 1 but some of the associated records were not loaded. Either make sure they are all loaded together with the parent record, or specify that the relationship is async (belongsTo({ async: true }))

Choosing an asynchronous or synchronous relationship depends on your application and the API. Personally, I lean toward making relationships synchronous as much as possible, which I have found to be the most clear and straightforward.

We've covered the basics of model relationships, but we haven't discussed how an API should return relationship data. We will look at that more in Chapter 3 – API Response Formats and Serializers.

Summary

We've gone through a simple example that covered fetching a collection of resources (even though the collection only had one cat resource). The example isn't comprehensive of all common data operations, but check out the Ember Guides to learn more about the basics of Ember Data like creating, updating, and deleting data. Let's now dive into adapters in the next chapter.

CHAPTER 2

Talking to APIs with Adapters

In the previous chapter, we looked at the architecture of Ember Data. We briefly discussed the role of the adapter and how it is responsible for figuring out how to make requests to an API. In this chapter, we'll look at the adapter and see how it works so that we can customize them in future chapters.

The adapter is responsible for figuring out how to make requests to an API. This includes determining the full URL based upon the model name and making the HTTP request using AJAX technologies like `$.ajax`, `fetch`, or `XMLHttpRequest`. If you wanted to store all of your data in Local Storage or communicate with a backend data store with WebSockets, this would also be the responsibility of the adapter.

We saw in the previous chapter that we can tell the adapter about our API using the `host` and `namespace` properties:

app/adapters/application.js

```javascript
import JSONAPIAdapter from '@ember-data/adapter/json-api';

export default class ApplicationAdapter extends JSONAPIAdapter
{
  host = 'http://localhost:8000';
  namespace = 'api/v1';
}
```

© David Tang 2021
D. Tang, *Pro Ember Data*, https://doi.org/10.1007/978-1-4842-6561-1_2

Ember Data ships with two adapters out of the box: the RESTAdapter and the JSONAPIAdapter. As you can see from the following diagram, the RESTAdapter extends from the base Adapter class, and the JSONAPIAdapter extends from the RESTAdapter.

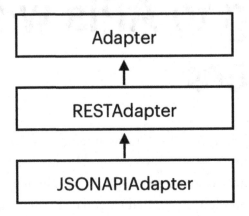

The Adapter class is an abstract class and provides a foundation for writing a custom adapter, which we will do in Chapter 5 – Writing an Adapter and Serializer from Scratch. In order to extend an adapter, it is important to understand how they work by default. Let's look at the RESTAdapter and then see how it differs from the JSONAPIAdapter.

The RESTAdapter

The RESTAdapter follows common REST conventions. Here is a list of common API operations and what methods they map to on the adapter:

Table 2-1.

Method	URL	Adapter Method	Description
GET	/api/cats	findAll()	Returns a collection of cat resources
GET	/api/cats/:id	findRecord()	Returns a single cat resource
POST	/api/cats	createRecord()	Creates a cat resource
PUT	/api/cats/:id	updateRecord()	Update a cat resource
DELETE	/api/cats/:id	deleteRecord()	Delete a cat resource
GET	/api/cats?color=black	query()	Returns a collection of resources
GET	/api/cats?color=black	queryRecord()	Returns a single resource

Notice how similar the adapter method names are to the store method names that you're probably familiar with. If you're familiar with the public methods on the store, you'll have a pretty good idea of what adapter methods are called, which can be useful when extending adapters.

Table 2-2.

Adapter Method	Invoked By
findAll()	store.findAll()
findRecord()	store.findRecord()
createRecord()	model.save()
updateRecord()	model.save() (if the model has an ID)
deleteRecord()	model.destroyRecord()
query()	store.query()
queryRecord()	store.queryRecord()

Each of these adapter methods makes a request following the REST conventions outlined earlier and returns a promise.

The preceding resource type, `cat`, is only a single word. If a resource type contains two words, the API path will be camelCased. For example, if our model was called `kitty-cat`, the URL path requested would be `/kittyCats`.

The `JSONAPIAdapter`

Ember Data supports the JSON:API specification[1] out of the box with the `JSONAPIAdapter`. If you aren't familiar with JSON:API, it is a specification for building APIs in JSON to increase team productivity by following shared conventions. This adapter extends the `RESTAdapter` so it has a lot of similarities. Let's look at the differences:

1. **The Accept and Content-Type Headers**

   On all requests, the `JSONAPIAdapter` sets the `Accept` header to `application/vnd.api+json` instead of `application/json`. The `Accept` header is used by clients to specify what type of content will be accepted. `application/vnd.api+json` is the media type, which is also referred to as a MIME type or content type, and it is used for JSON:API. The `vnd` denotes a vendor-specific MIME type. When data is sent to the server, such as when records are created or updated (POST, PUT, and PATCH requests), the `Content-Type` header is also set to `application/vnd.api+json`, which tells the server that the payload contains a JSON:API document so that it can parse it accordingly.

---

[1]`https://jsonapi.org/`

2. **Hyphenated URLs**

In JSON:API, resource types in URLs are hyphenated. Thus, the `JSONAPIAdapter` overrides the `pathForType()` adapter method so that resource paths are hyphenated as opposed to camelCased like in the `RESTAdapter`. For example, `findAll()` would trigger a GET request to `/api/kitty-cats` instead of `/api/kittyCats`.

3. **PATCH Instead of PUT**

When updating a record, the PATCH method is used instead of PUT. Why PATCH? The JSON:API specification states that using PUT to partially update a resource isn't allowed by the HTTP specification. PUT was instead meant for completely replacing a resource. For partial updates, PATCH should be used. In the past, PATCH wasn't well supported by HTTP clients, but now most of them do support it, and if they don't, there are workarounds. Whenever we update our records on the client and call `save()`, a PATCH request will be made.

4. **Loading Relationships**

By default, Ember Data will try and load related resources individually. For example, if a cat has three toys, and we try to access the cat's toys, a separate request will be made for each toy. If the cat has a lot of toys, this could result in quite a few requests, which may not be the most performant solution. Ember Data provides an option to group these requests into a single request, and this is where `RESTAdapter` and `JSONAPIAdapter` differ.

Imagine if we fetched a cat and got the following JSON:API response. Don't worry so much about this format yet, as we will look at it more in Chapter 3 – API Response Formats and Serializers:

```
{
  "data": [
    {
      "type": "cats",
      "id": 1,
      "attributes": {
        "name": "Frisky",
        "age": 10,
        "adopted": true,
        "birthday": "2005-11-05T13:15:30Z"
      },
      "relationships": {
        "toys": {
          "data": [
            {
              "id": 1,
              "type": "toys"
            },
            {
              "id": 2,
              "type": "toys"
            },
            {
              "id": 3,
              "type": "toys"
            }
          ]
        }
      }
    }
}
```

```
      }
  ]
}
```

This payload contains a single `cat` resource with an `id` of 1, and this cat has three toys containing ids 1, 2, and 3. This payload doesn't contain the actual data for the toys. It merely tells us that the cat has toys and what those ids are. We'd have to request that data if it was needed.

Let's say we want to display each of the cat's toys in our template:

```
{{#each cat.toys as |toy|}}
  <div>{{toy.name}}</div>
{{/each}}
```

Displaying each toy will cause the following requests to be made:

- GET `http://localhost:8000/api/v1/toys/1`

- GET `http://localhost:8000/api/v1/toys/2`

- GET `http://localhost:8000/api/v1/toys/3`

Feel free to update `server.js` with the following so that those requests succeed:

```
app.get('/api/v1/toys/:id', (request, response) => {
  const { id } = request.params;

  response.json({
    data: {
      type: 'toys',
      id,
      attributes: {
        name: `Toy ${id}`
      }
    }
  });
});
```

21

We can group these requests together with the `coalesceFindRequests` option:

```
import JSONAPIAdapter from '@ember-data/adapter/json-api';

export default class ApplicationAdapter extends JSONAPIAdapter
{
  host = 'http://localhost:8000';
  namespace = 'api/v1';
  coalesceFindRequests = true;
}
```

When using the `JSONAPIAdapter`, setting `coalesceFindRequests` to true will result in the following request instead:

```
GET http://localhost:8000/api/v1/toys?filter[id]=1,2,3
```

If we were using the `RESTAdapter`, assigning `coalesceFindRequests` to true would result in the following request:

```
GET http://localhost:8000/api/v1/toys?ids[]=1&ids[]=2&ids[]=3
```

Notice the difference in the structure of the query string parameters? JSON:API uses a `filter[attribute]` query string parameter for filtering where the value in brackets is the attribute that we want to filter on. The filter value is a comma-separated list. Check out the JSON:API specification for more about filtering.[2]

The ActiveModelAdapter

It's also worth mentioning the `ActiveModelAdapter`. This used to ship with Ember Data, but in Ember Data 2.x, it was removed and can be installed as an add-on.

---

[2]https://jsonapi.org/recommendations/#filtering

This adapter also extends the RESTAdapter and is really similar. The main difference with this adapter is that resource paths use underscores instead of camelCase, such as /api/kitty_cats.

To install this add-on, run the following:

```
ember install active-model-adapter
```

Then, import the adapter and extend it:

app/adapters/application.js

```
import ActiveModelAdapter from 'active-model-adapter';

export default class ApplicationAdapter extends
ActiveModelAdapter {
  // customizations
}
```

Background Reloading

Background reloading means the record in the store is initially returned to the caller but a request is made in the background to check for new data. This way, records in the store never get stale. If we'd like to control this behavior, there are a few methods in the adapter that we can override. These methods are already implemented in the base Adapter class:

Table 2-3.

Method	Returns	Description
shouldBackgroundReloadAll()	true	Reloads a record array after findAll resolves with a cached record array

(continued)

23

Table 2-3. (*continued*)

Method	Returns	Description
shouldBackgroundReloadRecord()	true	Reloads a record after findRecord resolves with a cached record
shouldReloadAll()	false	Reloads all records when store.findAll is called
shouldReloadRecord()	false	Reloads a record when store.findRecord is called

These methods simply return a boolean value. Both shouldReloadAll() and shouldReloadRecord() take precedence over shouldBackgroundReloadAll() and shouldBackgroundReloadRecord(). For example, if shouldReloadRecord() returns true, the record is always reloaded from the server whenever store.findRecord() is called, so there is no point in doing a background reload. The background reload methods are only checked by the store when it is returning either a cached record or cached record array.

Summary

In this chapter, we learned that the adapter is responsible for making requests to an API and that Ember Data comes with two adapters out of the box. Now that we know how the built-in adapters work, let's look at how to handle formatting data sent to and received from the server with serializers.

CHAPTER 3

API Response Formats and Serializers

A serializer in Ember Data is used to format data as it is transferred between the client and the server. When a serializer formats response data, this process is called *normalization*. In contrast, when a serializer formats data sent to the server, this process is called *serialization*.

Ember Data comes with three built-in serializers:

1. `JSONSerializer`

2. `RESTSerializer`

3. `JSONAPISerializer`

Each one of these serializers targets a specific API payload structure. In order to get a custom API working with Ember Data, it helps to understand the format that each of these serializers expects so that you can choose the one that matches the API as close as possible. Choosing a serializer that is the most similar to your API will likely reduce the number of customizations you will have to make.

© David Tang 2021

D. Tang, *Pro Ember Data*, https://doi.org/10.1007/978-1-4842-6561-1_3

The `JSONSerializer`

The `JSONSerializer`, not to be confused with the `JSONAPISerializer`, is a serializer that can be used for APIs with very simple payload structures. For example, let's say our application makes a request to `/api/contacts/1`. The expected JSON response is

```
{
  "id": 1,
  "fullName": "David Tang"
}
```

This resource object is simple and merely contains the resource's `id` and attributes in camelCase, which map to model attributes. There isn't any extra meta information.

When creating a resource, we would send

```
{
  "fullName": "David Tang"
}
```

When updating a resource, we would send

```
{
  "id": 1,
  "fullName": "David Tang"
}
```

What about endpoints like `/api/contacts` that return a collection of resources? As you might guess, the expected response contains an array of contact resources:

```
[
  { "id": 1, "fullName": "David Tang" },
  { "id": 2, "fullName": "Tom Dale" }
]
```

Here we have a model with hasMany and belongsTo relationships:

app/models/contact.js

```
import Model, { attr, hasMany, belongsTo } from '@ember-data/
model';

export default class ContactModel extends Model {
  @attr('string') fullName;
  @hasMany('pet', { async: true }) pets;
  @belongsTo('company', { async: true }) company;
}
```

In order for these relationships to be set up properly, the contact resource should contain the related data in the form of IDs:

```
{
  "id": 1,
  "fullName": "David Tang",
  "pets": [1, 2, 3],
  "company":  7
}
```

The pets and company attributes contain the IDs for each individual pet and company. Because we've declared our relationships as asynchronous, Ember Data will asynchronously load these related records when we need them, such as when accessing them off of a contact record in a template.

The RESTSerializer

The RESTSerializer extends from the JSONSerializer and expects a similar format but with a little more structure. It differs from the JSONSerializer, in that it introduces an extra root key that matches the model name. For example, if a request is made to /api/contacts/1, the expected JSON response is

```
{
  "contact": {
    "id": 1,
    "fullName": "David Tang",
    "pets": [1, 2, 3],
    "company":  7
  }
}
```

The root key is contact and matches the model name. Similarly if a request is made to /api/contacts, the expected JSON response is

```
{
  "contact": [
    {
      "id": 1,
      "fullName": "David Tang",
      "pets": [1, 2, 3],
      "company": 7
    },
    {
      "id": 2,
      "fullName": "Tom Dale",
      "pets": [4],
      "company": 7
    }
  ]
}
```

It's worth noting that the root key can also be in the plural form (i.e., contacts).

In the previous contact resource example using the JSONSerializer format, pets and company would have needed to be asynchronously loaded from the server or loaded into the store prior to accessing that related data. One of the benefits of using the RESTSerializer format is that it supports data sideloading, which allows us to include related records in the response of the primary data that is requested without duplication. For example, when a request is made to /api/contacts/1, a response with sideloaded data would look like the following:

```
{
  "contact": {
    "id": 1,
    "fullName": "David Tang",
    "pets": [1, 3],
    "company": 7
  },
  "pet": [
    { "id": 1, "name": "Fiona" },
    { "id": 3, "name": "Biscuit" }
  ],
  "company": [{ "id": 7, "name": "Company A" }]
}
```

The response has keys pet and company that correspond to the sideloaded data. This was not possible with the JSONSerializer format. Using sideloaded data also enables us to make our model relationships synchronous with a single request:

app/models/contact.js

```
import Model, { attr, hasMany, belongsTo } from '@ember-data/
model';

export default class ContactModel extends Model {
  @attr('string') fullName;
  @hasMany('pet', { async: false }) pets; // synchronous
  @belongsTo('company', { async: false }) company; // synchronous
}
```

If we wanted our relationships to be synchronous with the JSONSerializer, we would need to make sure that all companies and pets were loaded in the store prior to accessing the related records.

The JSONAPISerializer

Like the RESTSerializer, the JSONAPISerializer also extends from the JSONSerializer and it expects data to adhere to the JSON:API specification. Because Ember Data uses JSON:API internally to represent data, it is useful to know the basics of JSON:API even if your API isn't following JSON:API.

For an endpoint that returns a single resource, like /api/contacts/1, a JSON:API-compliant response looks like the following:

```
{
  "data": {
    "type": "contacts",
    "id": "1",
    "attributes": {
      "first-name": "David",
      "last-name": "Tang"
    }
  }
}
```

A JSON:API resource object must have the top-level members id and type. The type property contains the model name either in its singular or plural form. You'll find that the type is plural for all of the examples in the JSON:API specification. The resource's data is contained in the attributes property. Attributes are hyphenated and will map to camelCased attributes on our model. For example, first-name and last-name will map to firstName and lastName on our model as such:

app/models/contact.js

```
import Model, { attr } from '@ember-data/model';

export default class ContactModel extends Model {
  @attr('string') firstName;
  @attr('string') lastName;
}
```

For an endpoint that returns a collection of resources, such as /api/contacts, a JSON:API-compliant response would be the following:

```
{
  "data": [
    {
      "type": "contacts",
      "id": "1",
      "attributes": {
        "first-name": "David",
        "last-name": "Tang"
      }
    },
    {
      "type": "contacts",
      "id": "2",
```

31

```
      "attributes": {
        "first-name": "Tom",
        "last-name": "Dale"
      }
    }
  ]
}
```

Like before, there is a data key, but this time it contains an array instead of an object. Each element in the array is a resource object that matches the same structure as when fetching a single resource object, that is, an object with keys type, id, and attributes.

Relationships

Relationships are handled with the relationships key:

```
{
  "data": {
    "type": "contacts",
    "id": "1",
    "attributes": {
      "first-name": "David",
      "last-name": "Tang"
    },
    "relationships": {
      "pets": {
        "data": [
          { "type": "pets", "id": 1 },
          { "type": "pets", "id": 2 }
        ]
      },
```

```
      "company": {
        "data": {
          "type": "companies",
          "id": 1
        }
      }
    }
  }
}
```

In the preceding JSON, the `relationships` object is structured for a `hasMany` pet relationship and a `belongsTo` company relationship:

app/models/contact.js

```
import Model, { attr, hasMany, belongsTo } from '@ember-data/
model';

export default class ContactModel extends Model {
  @attr('string') firstName;
  @attr('string') lastName;
  @hasMany('pet') pets; // asynchronous
  @belongsTo('company') company; // asynchronous
}
```

Notice the form of the keys directly under `relationships`. The singularization or pluralization of these keys directly corresponds to our model relationships, `pets` and `company`. Don't confuse this with the singularization or pluralization of `type`, which can be either singular or plural.

Also notice that data/relationships/pets/data[1] is an array and data/relationships/company/data is an object. Each element in the data/relationships/pets/data array is a pet resource object, but there are no attributes. Same with data/relationships/company/data. These resource objects only contain the id and the type and specify that relationships exist. The pet and company resources would need to be loaded from the server or alternatively sideloaded.

Sideloading

Related resources can be sideloaded with the included key:

```
{
  "data": {
    "type": "contacts",
    "id": "1",
    "attributes": {
      "first-name":  "David",
      "last-name": "Tang"
    },
    "relationships": {
      "pets": {
        "data": [
          { "type": "pets", "id": 1 },
          { "type": "pets", "id": 2 }
        ]
      },
      "company": {
        "data": {
```

---

[1]JSON Pointer defines a string syntax for identifying a specific value within a JavaScript Object Notation (JSON) document.

```
            "type": "companies",
            "id": 1
          }
        }
      }
    },
    "included": [
      {
        "type": "pets",
        "id": "1",
        "attributes": {
          "name": "Fiona"
        }
      },
      {
        "type": "pets",
        "id": "2",
        "attributes": {
          "name": "Biscuit"
        }
      },
      {
        "type": "companies",
        "id": "1",
        "attributes": {
          "name": "Apple"
        }
      }
    ]
}
```

The included key is an array used for sideloading resources. The user resource with an id of 1 has two pet resources and one company resource declared under relationships. The data in the included array contains the associated resources using the same JSON:API resource object structure with keys for type, id, and attributes. Now our model relationships can be made synchronous:

app/models/contact.js

```
import Model, { attr, hasMany, belongsTo } from '@ember-data/
model';

export default class ContactModel extends Model {
  @attr('string') firstName;
  @attr('string') lastName;
  @hasMany('pet', { async: false }) pets; // synchronous
  @belongsTo('company', { async: false }) company;
                                         // synchronous
}
```

Normalized JSON:API

I mentioned earlier that Ember Data's internal format uses normalized JSON:API, which is why it helps to know JSON:API even if your API isn't using JSON:API. Normalized JSON:API is JSON:API with a few minor adjustments. When we normalize payloads, we are changing the structure of the payload to this normalized JSON:API format so that Ember Data can use it. Those minor adjustments are the following:

- type should always be in singular, dasherized form.

- Members (properties) should be camelCased.

The Base Serializer

It's worth mentioning that there is another serializer, `Serializer`. This serializer is an abstract class that `JSONSerializer` extends from. If your API is wildly different and one of the built-in serializers can't be used, then consider using this one. If you look at the source code for `Serializer`, there isn't much to it. It is a simple `EmberObject` with a few defaults. In the next chapter, we will write our own serializer from scratch that extends `Serializer` so we can get a better idea of how serializers work.

Using a Serializer

We've looked at the different formats that each serializer expects. To create a serializer with Ember CLI, we can use the following command:

```
ember generate serializer application
```

This command will generate an application-level serializer that will be used for all models. If an `application` serializer isn't generated, Ember Data will use the `JSONAPISerializer`. Alternatively, we can create serializers for specific models:

```
ember generate serializer <model-name>
```

In the next few chapters, we will use both model-specific and `application` serializers depending on the customization. If you think a customization will apply to all models, make it generic enough and put it in the `application` serializer. If the customization is specific to a certain model, put it in a model-specific serializer.

Summary

Ember Data ships with three serializers out of the box. Knowing the API formats that these serializers expect can help you determine which one most closely matches your API so that you can extend from that and ultimately do as little adapter and serializer customizations as possible. Now that we know the expected payload structures of the serializers included in Ember Data, let's look at a few common customizations in the next chapter.

CHAPTER 4

Common Adapter and Serializer Customizations

By now you have an understanding of the roles of the different parts of Ember Data. You're probably thinking, this is great, but I just want to get my API working with Ember Data already! That's what this chapter is for. Now I won't be able to cover every single edge case, but the goal of this chapter is to introduce you to methods and properties that are frequently overridden to get Ember Data working with a custom API.

Changing the RESTful URL Path

Not all APIs follow the RESTful URL conventions that Ember Data expects as discussed in Chapter 2 – Talking to APIs with Adapters. For example, what if our API's URL used the singular form of the resource instead of the plural, such as /contact/1 instead of /contacts/1? If all of our contact endpoints followed this singular convention, we could override the pathForType() method on a contact adapter:

app/adapters/contact.js

```
import ApplicationAdapter from './application';

export default class ContactAdapter extends ApplicationAdapter
{
  pathForType(modelName) {
    return modelName;
  }
}
```

Here we are returning the model name, which is already singular.

If all of the URLs in the API followed this singular resource path convention, we could put this logic in the `application` adapter:

app/adapters/application.js

```
import RESTAdapter from '@ember-data/adapter/rest';

export default class ApplicationAdapter extends RESTAdapter {
  pathForType(modelName) {
    return modelName;
  }
}
```

Changing the URL for Certain Operations

Now let's say we want to query for all contacts in a given city:

```
this.store.query('contact', {
  city: 'Los Angeles'
});
```

The default behavior in Ember Data is to make a GET request where the city is represented as a query string parameter, such as /api/contacts?city=Los+Angeles. However, let's say our endpoint expects

the city to be represented as a dynamic segment such as /api/contacts/
los-angeles. Because this really only pertains to contacts, we can create
a contact adapter to handle changing this URL. We'll first create our
application adapter:

app/adapters/application.js

```
import RESTAdapter from '@ember-data/adapter/rest';

export default class ApplicationAdapter extends RESTAdapter {
  host = 'http://myapi.com';
  namespace = 'api';
}
```

Next, we can override the urlForQuery() method. This method is
responsible for returning the URL whenever store.query() is called:

app/adapters/contact.js

```
import ApplicationAdapter from './application';
import { dasherize } from '@ember/string';

export default class ContactAdapter extends ApplicationAdapter
{
  urlForQuery(query, modelName) {
    let city = dasherize(query.city.toLowerCase());
    delete query.city;
    return '${this.host}/${this.namespace}/contacts/${city}';
  }
}
```

Adapters have similar methods for other common store operations
such as urlForCreateRecord(), urlForDeleteRecord(), and
urlForFindAll() to name a few.

Mapping Differently Named Payload Keys to Model Attributes

What happens if our API returns a payload with keys that aren't camelCased, which is the JavaScript convention? The keys might be snaked_cased or TitleCased or have mixed conventions. We could have our model attributes follow our API's stylistic and naming conventions, but that might make our JavaScript code less intuitive and consistent. Let's imagine we have the following payload:

```
[
  {
    "id": 1,
    "first_name": "David",
    "years_old": 40
  }
]
```

We can map payload keys to model attributes and vice versa using attrs on the serializer:

app/serializers/contact.js

```
import JSONSerializer from '@ember-data/serializer/json';

export default class ContactSerializer extends JSONSerializer {
  attrs = {
    firstName: 'first_name',
    age: 'years_old'
  };
}
```

The first_name payload key will get mapped to the firstName attribute on the model. Similarly, the years_old payload key will get mapped to the age attribute on the model. When data is serialized and sent back to the server, these attributes will get mapped back to their original keys.

Mapping Foreign Keys to Relationships

Using `attrs` can be useful if you want to map specific payload keys to model attributes, but what if our API exposes foreign keys that follow the convention XXX_id, which are intended for `belongsTo` relationships? This is a pretty common convention in relational databases that can get exposed in APIs. For example, every `contact` might have an attribute `company_id` as opposed to `company`:

```
{
  "contact": {
    "id": 1,
    "name": "David",
    "company_id": 3
  }
}
```

Creating a model-specific serializer and specifying the attribute mappings in `attrs` for every single model could get cumbersome. Instead, a better way to handle this is to override `keyForRelationship()` in the serializer:

app/serializers/application.js

```
import RESTSerializer from '@ember-data/serializer/rest';

export default class ApplicationSerializer extends
RESTSerializer {
  keyForRelationship(key, relationship) {
    if (relationship === 'belongsTo') {
      return '${key}_id';
    }

    return super.keyForRelationship(key, relationship);
  }
}
```

Now a JSON payload containing foreign keys for each contact resource, like company_id, can map to the corresponding belongsTo relationships on our contact model:

app/models/contact.js

```
import Model, { attr, belongsTo } from '@ember-data/model';

export default class ContactModel extends Model {
  @attr('string') name;
  @belongsTo('company') company;
}
```

Setting the Primary Key

Ember Data expects every record to have an attribute called id. If a record needs to use another key as its id, you can override the primaryKey property:

app/serializers/contact.js

```
import RESTSerializer from '@ember-data/serializer/rest';

export default class ContactSerializer extends RESTSerializer {
  primaryKey = 'ssn'; // social security number
}
```

Here we are changing the id for the contact model to be ssn instead. We can access id on any contact record to access ssn. If all records use a property like _id as the id such as in MongoDB, then override primaryKey in an application serializer so that it applies to all models.

Normalizing Responses

Let's say we call store.findAll('contact') and the sample JSON from
Chapter 1 - Ember Data Overview is returned:

```
{
  "data": [
    { "id": 1, "firstName": "Yehuda" },
    { "id": 2, "firstName": "Tom" }
  ]
}
```

None of the built-in serializers in Ember Data work with API payloads
in this format by default. This format is similar to the format expected by
the JSONSerializer, except there is a root data key. We just need to extract
data, and we can do that by overriding normalizeResponse():

app/serializers/contact.js

```
import JSONSerializer from '@ember-data/serializer/json';

export default class ContactSerializer extends JSONSerializer {
  normalizeResponse(store, primaryModelClass, payload, id,
  requestType) {
    return super.normalizeResponse(
      store,
      primaryModelClass,
      payload.data,
      id,
      requestType
    );
  }
}
```

The normalizeResponse() method is used to normalize a payload from the server to a normalized JSON:API document, which we discussed in Chapter 3 – API Response Formats and Serializers. Rather than creating the normalized JSON:API directly, we can instead modify the payload to fit the JSONSerializer structure and call the same method on the parent class with super which will return normalized JSON:API for us. This approach requires much less code, as opposed to manipulating the payload to the normalized JSON:API format ourselves. If you'd like to see the normalized JSON:API, do the following:

app/serializers/contact.js

```
import JSONSerializer from '@ember-data/serializer/json';
export default class ContactSerializer extends JSONSerializer {
  normalizeResponse(store, primaryModelClass, payload, id,
  requestType) {
    let json = super.normalizeResponse(
      store,
      primaryModelClass,
      payload.data,
      id,
      requestType
    );

    console.log(JSON.stringify(json));

    return json;
  }
}
```

You should see the following normalized JSON:API logged to the console:

```
{
  "data": [
    {
      "id": "1",
      "type": "contact",
      "attributes": { "firstName": "Yehuda" },
      "relationships": {}
    },
    {
      "id": "2",
      "type": "contact",
      "attributes": { "firstName": "Tom" },
      "relationships": {}
    }
  ],
  "included": []
}
```

Notice how this format matches the normalized JSON:API format we discussed in Chapter 3 – API Response Formats and Serializers? That is, type is in singular, dasherized form and properties like firstName are in camelCase.

Another way we can work with this response is by changing that data key in the payload to the model name and using the RESTSerializer:

app/serializers/contact.js

```
import RESTSerializer from '@ember-data/serializer/rest';

export default class ContactSerializer extends RESTSerializer {
  normalizeResponse(store, primaryModelClass, payload, id,
  requestType) {
    let newPayload = {};
    newPayload[primaryModelClass.modelName] = payload.data;
```

```
  return super.normalizeResponse(
    store,
    primaryModelClass,
    newPayload,
    id,
    requestType
  );
  }
}
```

If you recall from Chapter 3 – API Response Formats and Serializers, on the RESTSerializer, the root key is the model name and it can be either singular or plural. In the preceding code, the singularized model name is used for the root key. Similar to before, we will change the payload structure in normalizeResponse() to match the current serializer's expected format and then call super.normalizeResponse().

Normalizing Responses by Store Call

In the previous section, we overrode normalizeResponse() to handle that data key in our payloads. This would apply to all of our contact payloads for the different RESTful operations. What if that data key only existed for certain RESTful endpoints? We could add some conditional logic to normalizeResponse(), but that can get messy. If we only wanted to extract that data key when we call store.findAll(), we can instead override a specific serializer method for when store.findAll() is called. This method is normalizeFindAllResponse():

app/serializers/contact.js

```
import JSONSerializer from '@ember-data/serializer/json';

export default class ContactSerializer extends JSONSerializer {
```

```
normalizeFindAllResponse(store, primaryModelClass, payload,
id, requestType) {
  return super.normalizeFindAllResponse(
    store,
    primaryModelClass,
    payload.data,
    id,
    requestType
  );
 }
}
```

This is exactly the same as before, but instead of overriding
normalizeResponse(), normalizeFindAllResponse() was overridden. In
the preceding code, JSONSerializer was used, but RESTSerializer could
have been used as we did in the last section.

Table 4-1 shows other serializer normalization methods and how they
get invoked.

Table 4-1. *Serializer Normalization Methods*

Store or Model Call	Serializer Method
store.findAll()	normalizeFindAllResponse()
store.findRecord()	normalizeFindRecordResponse()
model.save()	normalizeCreateRecordResponse()
store.deleteRecord()	normalizeDeleteRecordResponse()
store.query()	normalizeQueryResponse()
store.queryRecord()	normalizeQueryRecordResponse()
	normalizeFindBelongsToResponse()
	normalizeFindHasManyResponse()

`normalizeFindBelongsToResponse()` and
`normalizeFindHasManyResponse()` get called when `belongsTo` and
`hasMany` relationships are requested.

Normalizing Single Resource Objects

Let's say our `contact` API payloads fit one of the built-in serializer formats.
For example, `/api/contacts` might return

```
[
  {
    "id": 1,
    "name": { "first": "John", "last": "Doe" }
  },
  {
    "id": 2,
    "name": { "first": "Jane", "last": "Doe" }
  }
]
```
and `/api/contacts/:id` might return
```
{
  "id": 1,
  "name": { "first": "John", "last": "Doe" }
}
```

Both of these payloads fit the `JSONSerializer` format, but `name` on
each contact is a nested object. To concatenate `name.first` and `name.`
`last`, we could override the `normalize()` method, which normalizes a
single resource object in a payload into a JSON:API object:

app/serializers/contact.js

```
import JSONSerializer from '@ember-data/serializer/json';

export default class ContactSerializer extends JSONSerializer {
  normalize(modelClass, resourceHash, prop) {
    let { name } = resourceHash;
    return {
      data: {
        id: resourceHash.id,
        type: 'contact',
        attributes: {
          name: '${name.first} ${name.last}'
        }
      }
    };
  }
}
```

Inside the `normalize()` method, we've taken each `contact` and normalized it into the JSON:API format. For a single resource endpoint like `/api/contacts/:id`, the `normalize()` method will get called once. For an endpoint that returns a collection of resources such as `/api/contacts`, `normalize()` will get called for each resource object.

Rather than turning each `contact` into JSON:API ourselves, we can achieve the same result more efficiently by calling the same method on the parent class using `super`:

app/serializers/contact.js

```
import JSONSerializer from '@ember-data/serializer/json';

export default class ContactSerializer extends JSONSerializer {
  normalize(modelClass, resourceHash, prop) {
    let { name } = resourceHash;
```

```
    resourceHash.name = '${name.first} ${name.last}';
    return super.normalize(...arguments);
  }
}
```

In the preceding code, we are manipulating each object passed into
normalize() as resourceHash and then calling the original normalize()
method on the parent class with super. Not only does this approach
require less code, we're letting Ember Data handle the specifics of
JSON:API and other scenarios that we're not considering for more
complicated responses.

Summary

In this chapter, I introduced some frequent customizations I have made
in adapters and serializers to get Ember Data working with a custom
API. At this point, maybe this chapter was enough to fix your current
problem. If so, I'm glad it helped! However, if you're still a little confused
on how adapters and serializers work together, continue on to the next two
chapters where we will build two adapters and a serializer from scratch.

CHAPTER 5

Writing an Adapter and Serializer from Scratch

In this chapter, we will learn how to write an adapter and serializer from scratch. If you didn't find a technique in the previous chapter to get your API working with Ember Data, then this chapter and the next will give you more insight into how an adapter and a serializer work together and expose you to some of the core methods of each. The process of writing an adapter and serializer from scratch will help you find the right methods to override for your particular edge case. Furthermore, if you need to work with a wildly different API, then you will know how to write your own!

We will start by rebuilding a simplified version of the `RESTAdapter` and `RESTSerializer` for the standard CRUD operations.

Setup

I've created a simple contact application that performs all of the standard CRUD operations. The code for this application can be found in the chapter-5 folder of the source code for this book. We will use this application as a way of testing our custom adapters and serializer.

The API is set up using Ember CLI Mirage (`www.ember-cli-mirage.com/`). If you aren't familiar with Mirage, it is a library that lets us simulate a backend.

Our Custom Adapter and Serializer

To start, let's create our custom adapter called `my-rest` that extends from the base adapter class `Adapter`:

```
ember generate adapter my-rest
```

app/adapters/my-rest.js

```
import Adapter from '@ember-data/adapter';

export default class MyRESTAdapter extends Adapter {}
```

Next, create an `application` adapter that extends from our custom adapter with an `api` namespace:

```
ember generate adapter application
```

```
import MyRESTAdapter from './my-rest';

export default class ApplicationAdapter extends MyRESTAdapter {
  namespace = 'api';
}
```

Let's do the same for the serializer. We'll create a custom serializer called `my-rest` that extends from the base serializer class `Serializer`:

```
ember generate serializer my-rest
```

app/serializers/my-rest.js

```
import Serializer from '@ember-data/serializer';

export default class MyRESTSerializer extends Serializer {}
```

Lastly, create an `application` serializer that extends from our custom serializer:

```
ember generate serializer application
```

app/serializers/application.js

```
import MyRESTSerializer from './my-rest';

export default class ApplicationSerializer extends
MyRESTSerializer {}
```

Now that we have an `application` adapter extending from our custom adapter and an `application` serializer extending from our custom serializer, let's move on to the implementation and get `store.findAll()` working.

Finding All Records

Serve the test application, visit `http://localhost:4200/contacts`, and open up the browser console. You will notice that the page throws an error. This is because our `application` adapter and serializer no longer extend from the built-in `RESTAdapter` and `RESTSerializer`, respectively.

Let's start by implementing the necessary methods to get the `/contacts` page working. If you look at the `contacts` route, you will see the following:

app/routes/contacts.js

```
import Route from '@ember/routing/route';

export default class ContactsRoute extends Route {
  model() {
    return this.store.findAll('contact');
  }
}
```

Let's take a closer look at the error message.

Error   You tried to load all records, but your adapter does not implement `findAll`.

Remember, the adapter is responsible for figuring out how to make requests to an API. As discussed in Chapter 2 – Talking to APIs with Adapters, `store.findAll()` calls `adapter.findAll()` behind the scenes. The `findAll()` method on the adapter is used to find all records for a given type. Let's go ahead and implement that:

app/adapters/my-rest.js

```
import Adapter from '@ember-data/adapter';
import { pluralize } from 'ember-inflector';
import $ from 'jquery';

export default class MyRESTAdapter extends Adapter {
  findAll(store, type, neverSet, snapshotRecordArray) {
    let url = '/${this.namespace}/${pluralize(type.
    modelName)}';
    return $.get(url);
  }
}
```

The `findAll()` method on the adapter gets passed a few arguments, but the one we are particularly interested in is `type`, which contains the model class which has a property containing the model's name. Here we are taking the model name and pluralizing it so that a GET request is made to `/api/contacts`. If we look at the console, we're still getting an error:

Error   serializer.normalizeResponse is not a function

The normalizeResponse() method must be implemented on the serializer, and it is responsible for normalizing a payload from the server into a JSON:API document. As mentioned before, Ember Data uses JSON:API internally, even if your API does not. Currently, our Mirage backend is returning a list of contacts like this:

```
{
  "contacts": [
    {
      "id": "1",
      "name": "Tom",
      "phoneNumber": "(123) 456-7890"
    }
  ]
}
```

Let's go ahead and implement normalizeResponse() so that it takes this payload and returns a JSON:API document. If you aren't familiar with the basic JSON:API structure, go back to Chapter 3 – API Response Formats and Serializers and read the section "The JSONAPISerializer":

app/serializers/my-rest.js

```
import Serializer from '@ember-data/serializer';

export default class MyRESTSerializer extends Serializer {
  normalizeResponse(store, primaryModelClass, payload, id,
  requestType) {
    return {
      data: payload.contacts.map((resource) => {
        return {
          id: resource.id,
```

```
      type: 'contact',
      attributes: resource
    };
   })
  };
 }
}
```

The normalizeResponse() method has several parameters, but the one we are interested in is payload. Now there are a lot of methods in the serializer, but if you have to remember one, normalizeResponse() is it. If you ever need to modify the payload before it gets into Ember Data, you can always override this method. There are other methods you can override to more efficiently manipulate the payload, but know that you can always use this one. Here we created the root data key that contains a list of contacts. Each contact is restructured to be JSON:API compliant, containing id, type, and attributes. Check the page again. Everything works!

We aren't finished yet. If we tried to use this serializer with other models, it would fail because we have hard-coded contact in normalizeResponse(). Let's modify this to make it more generic:

app/serializers/my-rest.js

```
import Serializer from '@ember-data/serializer';
import { pluralize } from 'ember-inflector';

export default class MyRESTSerializer extends Serializer {
  normalizeResponse(store, primaryModelClass, payload, id,
  requestType) {
    let pluralizedModelName = pluralize(primaryModelClass.
    modelName);
```

```
  return {
    data: payload[pluralizedModelName].map((resource) => {
      return {
        id: resource.id,
        type: primaryModelClass.modelName,
        attributes: resource
      };
    })
  };
  }
}
```

Here we have utilized the `primaryModelClass` argument which is the model class for the records we are finding. We picked off the `modelName` and pluralized it to dynamically access the data from the root payload key. Loading the list of contacts still works! Let's move on to `findRecord()`.

Finding a Single Record

If we try clicking a contact, we'll see that we get an error. In the `contacts.contact` route, we are fetching a single contact by the `id` dynamic segment:

app/routes/contacts/contact.js

```
import Route from '@ember/routing/route';

export default class ContactsContactRoute extends Route {
  model(params) {
    return this.store.findRecord('contact', params.id);
  }
}
```

We need to update our adapter to get `store.findRecord()` working. The adapter method that maps to `store.findRecord()` is, you guessed it, `findRecord()`. Let's implement that:

app/adapters/my-rest.js

```
import Adapter from '@ember-data/adapter';
import { pluralize } from 'ember-inflector';
import $ from 'jquery';

export default class MyRESTAdapter extends Adapter {
  // ...
  findRecord(store, type, id, snapshot) {
    let url = '/${this.namespace}/${pluralize(type.
    modelName)}/${id}';
    return  $.get(url);
  }
}
```

This implementation is similar to the findAll() implementation that we did earlier, but this time the id of the record we are trying to find is tacked onto the end of the URL. Now, it still isn't working yet. The console outputs the following error:

Error   Cannot read property 'map' of undefined

This error is now concerning the payload. Previously, we implemented normalizeResponse() in the serializer and we used Array.prototype.map() to turn the payload into a JSON:API-compliant document. However, the GET /api/contacts/:id endpoint returns a single resource, not an array. The payload looks like this for /api/contacts/1:

```
{
  "contact": {
    "id": "1",
    "name": "Tom",
    "phoneNumber": "(123) 456-7890"
  }
}
```

To accommodate a single resource response, we can do this a few different ways. Remember how I said if you were to remember one serializer method, it should be normalizeResponse()? Well, we can add some logic to this method to test whether an object or an array comes back:

app/serializers/my-rest.js

```javascript
import Serializer from '@ember-data/serializer';
import { pluralize } from 'ember-inflector';

export default class MyRESTSerializer extends Serializer {
  normalizeResponse(store, primaryModelClass, payload, id,
  requestType) {
    let { modelName } = primaryModelClass;
    let pluralizedModelName = pluralize(modelName);

    if (Array.isArray(payload[pluralizedModelName])) {
      return {
        data: payload[pluralizedModelName].map((resource) => {
          return {
            id: resource.id,
            type: modelName,
            attributes: resource
          };
        })
      };
    }

    let resource = payload[modelName];

    return {
      data: {
        id: resource.id,
        type: modelName,
```

```
        attributes: resource
      }
    };
  }
}
```

With the preceding code, now we can click a single contact. This implementation is still not ideal though. We have some duplicated code for generating a JSON:API resource object. It turns out there is a method dedicated for normalizing a single resource object called normalize(). The normalize() method takes the type (the model class) and the resource object. Let's clean this up a bit to do just that:

app/serializers/my-rest.js

```
import Serializer from '@ember-data/serializer';
import { pluralize } from 'ember-inflector';

export default class MyRESTSerializer extends Serializer {
  normalizeResponse(store, primaryModelClass, payload, id,
  requestType) {
    let { modelName } = primaryModelClass;
    let pluralizedModelName = pluralize(modelName);

    if (Array.isArray(payload[pluralizedModelName])) {
      return {
        data: payload[pluralizedModelName].map((resource) => {
          return this.normalize(primaryModelClass, resource);
        })
      };
    }
```

```
    return {
      data: this.normalize(primaryModelClass, payload[modelName])
    };
  }

  normalize(typeClass, hash) {
    return {
      id: hash.id,
      type: typeClass.modelName,
      attributes:  hash
    };
  }
}
```

In the preceding code, the normalize() method is used to convert a single resource object that looks like this:

```
{
  "id": 1,
  "name": "Tom",
  "phoneNumber": "(123) 456-7890"
}
```

into a JSON:API resource that looks like this:

```
{
  "id": 1,
  "type": "contact",
  "attributes": {
    "name": "Tom",
    "phoneNumber": "(123) 456-7890"
  }
}
```

Revisiting `normalizeResponse()`

Before we move on to creating records, let's revisit `normalizeResponse()`
on the serializer. If we were to take a look at the actual implementation of
`normalizeResponse()`[1], we'd see something like this:

```
import Serializer from '@ember-data/serializer';

export default Serializer.extend({
  // ...
  normalizeResponse(store, primaryModelClass, payload, id,
  requestType) {
    switch (requestType) {
      case 'findRecord':
        return this.normalizeFindRecordResponse(...arguments);
      case 'queryRecord':
        return this.normalizeQueryRecordResponse(...arguments);
      case 'findAll':
        return this.normalizeFindAllResponse(...arguments);
      case 'findBelongsTo':
        return this.normalizeFindBelongsToResponse(...
        arguments);
      case 'findHasMany':
        return this.normalizeFindHasManyResponse(...arguments);
      case 'findMany':
        return this.normalizeFindManyResponse(...arguments);
      case 'query':
        return this.normalizeQueryResponse(...arguments);
      case 'createRecord':
        return this.normalizeCreateRecordResponse(...arguments);
```

---

[1]https://github.com/emberjs/data/blob/v3.21.0/packages/serializer/
addon/json.js#L239

```
        case 'deleteRecord':
          return this.normalizeDeleteRecordResponse(...arguments);
        case 'updateRecord':
          return this.normalizeUpdateRecordResponse(...arguments);
      }
   }
});
```

Ember Data implements normalizeResponse() by delegating to a normalization method for a specific request type. Whenever store. findRecord() is called, the normalizeFindRecordResponse() method on the serializer is called; whenever store.findAll() is called, the normalizeFindAllResponse() method on the serializer is called; and so on and so forth. If we need a custom normalization method for a specific requestType, we can override one of these normalization methods.

Furthermore, if we wanted to handle all responses that return a collection of resources one way and a single resource another way, there are dedicated methods for those too. These methods are normalizeArrayResponse() and normalizeSingleResponse(). In fact, each of the requestType-specific normalization methods calls either normalizeArrayResponse() or normalizeSingleResponse() behind the scenes. Here is the execution flow (read from left to right):

```
{width="100%"}
| normalizeFindAllResponse()       | normalizeArrayResponse()  |                            |                            |
| normalizeFindRecordResponse()    | normalizeSingleResponse() |                            |                            |
| normalizeCreateRecordResponse()  | normalizeSaveResponse()   | normalizeSingleResponse()  |                            |
| normalizeDeleteRecordResponse()  | normalizeSaveResponse()   | normalizeSingleResponse()  |                            |
| normalizeUpdateRecordResponse()  | normalizeSaveResponse()   | normalizeSingleResponse()  |                            |
| normalizeQueryResponse()         | normalizeArrayResponse()  |                            |                            |
| normalizeQueryRecordResponse()   | normalizeSingleResponse() |                            |                            |
| normalizeFindBelongsToResponse() | normalizeSingleResponse() |                            |                            |
| normalizeFindHasManyResponse()   | normalizeArrayResponse()  |                            |                            |
```

Hopefully, this provides more insight into how normalization works in serializers.

Now that we can fetch data with `store.findAll()` and `store.findRecord()`, let's move on to the implementation for creating records.

Creating Records

Let's move on to creating records. Go ahead and visit `http://localhost:4200/contacts/new`. Fill out and submit the form for a new contact. You should see the following error:

Error   You tried to update a record but your adapter (for contact) does not implement `createRecord`

To create a record, we need to use `store.createRecord()`. This doesn't save the record though. To save the record, `save()` needs to be called on the record to persist those changes via a `POST /api/contacts` request, for example:

app/controllers/contacts/new.js

```
let contact = this.store.createRecord('contact', {
  name: this.name,
  phoneNumber: this.phoneNumber
});
```

```
contact.save();
```

The adapter method that gets called from `model.save()` is `createRecord()`. Our API expects a JSON payload to contain the data under a root key that matches the model name, similar to when we fetch a single record:

```
{
  "contact": {
    "name": "David",
    "phoneNumber": "(310) 123-4567"
  }
}
```

Here is an implementation of createRecord():

app/adapters/my-rest.js

```
import Adapter from '@ember-data/adapter';
import { pluralize } from 'ember-inflector';
import $ from 'jquery';

export default class MyRESTAdapter extends Adapter {
  // ...
  createRecord(store, type, snapshot) {
    let data = {};
    let serializer = store.serializerFor(type.modelName);
    serializer.serializeIntoHash(data, type, snapshot);

    return $.ajax({
      type: 'POST',
      url: '/${this.namespace}/${pluralize(type.modelName)}',
      data: JSON.stringify(data)
    });
  }
}
```

Inside createRecord(), a POST request is made using the pluralized model name to create the endpoint, such as /api/contacts, so that it is reusable for other models. How do we get the data to send? The data is contained within the snapshot argument. The snapshot argument is an instance of Snapshot, and it represents a record at a given moment in time. We'll discuss this more later. For now, just know that it is an object that contains the record we are saving.

Remember, the role of a serializer is to format data sent to and received from the server. Instead of formatting the snapshot data in the adapter, which we could do, we should do this in the serializer. To get access to our model's serializer, we can call the serializerFor() method on the store, giving it the model name. Next, serializers have a serializeIntoHash() method that can be called to format the request payload data. In this case, we are using serializeIntoHash() to build the data variable, which is modified by reference. We will implement this method in a moment. The type and snapshot arguments are also passed along. This data variable becomes our stringified JSON payload.

Lastly, we need to implement the serializeIntoHash() method on our serializer so that the data sent to the server matches the format expected by the backend:

app/serializers/my-rest.js

```
import Serializer from '@ember-data/serializer';
import { pluralize } from 'ember-inflector';

export default class MyRESTSerializer extends Serializer {
  // ...
  serializeIntoHash(hash, typeClass, snapshot) {
    let serializedData = {};

    snapshot.eachAttribute((name) => {
      serializedData[name] = snapshot.attr(name);
    });

    hash[typeClass.modelName] = serializedData;
  }
}
```

Our implementation of the `serializeIntoHash()` method looks at the model data contained in the snapshot and generates the payload the API expected. Snapshots have an `eachAttribute()` method that can be used to iterate through all the attributes on the model. We can get access to a record's attribute using `snapshot.attr()`. In the preceding code, we are iterating over all the attributes and setting them onto `serializedData` which will get sent to the server.

You might be wondering, "why did the Ember Data team create this extra snapshot object instead of using the record?" As I mentioned earlier, a snapshot is a class in Ember Data that represents a record at a given moment in time. When working with records, you can inspect asynchronous relationships, and if those relationships are not loaded, Ember Data will trigger a request to fetch that data. Unlike with regular records, a snapshot is an object that represents a record that can be inspected without causing side effects, like triggering requests. The snapshot has only a few properties and methods on it that you'll likely use, as shown in Table 5-1.

Table 5-1.

Snapshot Property/Method	Description
snapshot.id	Gets the ID of the record
snapshot.attr('name')	Gets an attribute of the record
snapshot.hasMany('emails')	Gets a hasMany relationship for the record. Returns another snapshot
snapshot.belongsTo('company')	Gets a belongsTo relationship for the record. Returns another snapshot
snapshot.record	Gets the original record
snapshot.eachAttribute(callback, binding)	Iterates through all model attributes and invokes the callback on each attribute

Now if you were to look at the source code for the RESTSerializer, it actually breaks up this functionality into two separate methods: serializeIntoHash() and serialize(). We can adjust our implementation to match what Ember Data is doing a little more closely:

app/serializers/my-rest.js

```
import Serializer from '@ember-data/serializer';
import { pluralize } from 'ember-inflector';

export default class MyRESTSerializer extends Serializer {
  // ...
  serializeIntoHash(hash, typeClass, snapshot) {
    hash[typeClass.modelName] = this.serialize(snapshot);
  }

  serialize(snapshot) {
    let serializedData = {};

    snapshot.eachAttribute((name) => {
      serializedData[name] = snapshot.attr(name);
    });

    return serializedData;
  }
}
```

The serialize() method is responsible for grabbing the data out of the snapshot and formatting it as needed, and the serializeIntoHash() method is responsible for customizing the root payload key.

Great! We can now find all records, find a single record, and create records. Let's continue on and handle updating records.

Updating a Record

Go ahead and click a contact. You will see a modal pop up that allows us to edit a contact.

Now that we've implemented `createRecord()`, `updateRecord()` is fairly similar. The two differences are the URL and the request type. First, the URL includes the `id` of the record to update, such as `/api/contacts/1` instead of `/api/contacts`. Second, the PUT HTTP method is used instead of POST. That's really it.

If we try and submit the form, we'll get the following error:

Error   You tried to update a record but your adapter (for contact) does not implement `updateRecord`

Let's go ahead and do that:

app/adapters/my-rest.js

```
import Adapter from '@ember-data/adapter';
import { pluralize } from 'ember-inflector';
import $ from 'jquery';

export default class MyRESTAdapter extends Adapter {
  updateRecord(store, type, snapshot) {
    let data = {};
    let serializer = store.serializerFor(type.modelName);

    serializer.serializeIntoHash(data, type, snapshot);

    return  $.ajax({
      type: 'PUT',
      url: '/${this.namespace}/${pluralize(type.
      modelName)}/${snapshot.id}',
```

```
    data: JSON.stringify(data)
  });
  }
}
```

We have to make one small adjustment to the serializer, specifically the serialize() method. Currently when a record is serialized, a plain object is created with all of the model's attributes, but the id isn't included if one is present. We'll add a check in there so that when a snapshot has an id, the id will be included in the serialized payload as well:

app/serializers/my-rest.js

```
import Serializer from '@ember-data/serializer';
import { pluralize } from 'ember-inflector';

export default class MyRESTSerializer extends Serializer {
  // ...
  serializeIntoHash(hash, typeClass, snapshot) {
    hash[typeClass.modelName] = this.serialize(snapshot);
  }

  serialize(snapshot) {
    let serializedData = {};

    if (snapshot.id) {
      serializedData.id = snapshot.id;
    }

    snapshot.eachAttribute((name) => {
      serializedData[name] = snapshot.attr(name);
    });

    return serializedData;
  }
}
```

That's it for updating records! Now that we can update records, let's continue on so that we can delete records.

Deleting a Record

Go ahead and click "Delete" for one of the contacts in the table. You should see the following error:

Error   You tried to update a record but your adapter (for contact) does not implement deleteRecord

---

To delete a contact, we need to make a DELETE request to /contacts/:id and the API will return an empty response. To make this request, we can call destroyRecord() on our model. Calling destroyRecord() on the model maps to deleteRecord() on the adapter. Let's implement that:

app/adapters/my-rest.js

```
import Adapter from '@ember-data/adapter';
import { pluralize } from 'ember-inflector';
import $ from 'jquery';

export default class MyRESTAdapter extends Adapter {
  // ...
  deleteRecord(store, type, snapshot) {
    return $.ajax({
      type: 'DELETE',
      url: '/${this.namespace}/${pluralize(type.
      modelName)}/${snapshot.id }'
    });
  }
}
```

In deleteRecord(), an AJAX request is made with the DELETE HTTP method to the same URL that we created in findRecord() and updateRecord(). Give it a shot, and you should see everything working as expected.

Congratulations! You've completed a custom REST adapter and serializer for the standard CRUD operations!

Summary

In this chapter, we looked at how to write our own adapter and serializer from scratch, starting from the base classes that Ember Data provides. There are other methods in the adapter and serializer that were not covered in this chapter. While we could continue going over every adapter and serializer method, what we did cover should give you the necessary insight into how these two core pieces of Ember Data work together. When you do you need more functionality, finding the right adapter or serializer method in the documentation should be a breeze. In the next chapter, we will continue with the same application and change our backend to Local Storage by simply swapping the adapter, since the adapter is responsible for figuring out how to get data and where to send it for storage.

CHAPTER 6

Swapping the API with Local Storage

We now know how to write an adapter and serializer from scratch as we learned in the last chapter. Imagine we've been tasked with swapping our backend to Local Storage. We know that adapters are responsible for figuring out how to talk to a backend via a RESTful API. They figure out how to retrieve data and where to send data for storage. In this chapter, we will swap out our custom RESTAdapter with our own Local Storage adapter, and our application should continue to work seamlessly.

Creating an Empty Adapter

To start, let's create a new empty adapter:

```
ember generate adapter local-storage
```

app/adapters/local-storage.js

```
import Adapter from '@ember-data/adapter';

export default class LocalStorageAdapter extends Adapter {}
```

Next, we'll update our `application` adapter to extend from our Local Storage adapter:

app/adapters/application.js

```
import LocalStorageAdapter from './local-storage';

export default class ApplicationAdapter extends
LocalStorageAdapter {
  namespace = 'api';
}
```

The `namespace` property is still going to be used but for the storage key in Local Storage to hold all of our data. Because Local Storage does not store JavaScript objects, we will need to stringify a JSON using `JSON.stringify()` when we persist our data. When we read the data out of Local Storage, we will parse it using `JSON.parse()`. The data will be stored in Local Storage structured like the following:

```
{
  "contacts": [],
  "dogs": [],
  "cats": []
}
```

We will use a simple object where the keys correspond to the pluralized model name and will contain a list of all objects of that type. You might want to throw some data into Local Storage before we start. Run the following to do so:

```
localStorage.setItem(
  'api',
  JSON.stringify({
    contacts: [
      { id: '1', name: 'Tom', phoneNumber: '(123) 456-7890' },
```

```
  { id: '2', name: 'Leah', phoneNumber: '(987) 456-7890' },
  { id: '3', name: 'Yehuda', phoneNumber: '(456) 456-7890'
}
  ]
})
);
```

To see the data in Local Storage, open up the *Application* panel in Chrome Developer Tools and click *Local Storage*. You will see all of the stringified JSON data under the Local Storage key *api*.

Now let's start the implementation of findAll().

Implementing findAll()

Let's look at the requirements before we implement findAll() on our adapter. First, findAll() expects a promise to be returned. In our custom RESTAdapter, we were returning the promise from $.get(). Because Local Storage is synchronous and doesn't return a promise, we can use Ember's Promise library, RSVP[1], to create one that resolves with the data. Second, the data that our promise resolves needs to be structured the same as the Mirage backend that we were using in our custom RESTAdapter so that we preserve this method's API and can continue to use our custom RESTSerializer.

Here is the full implementation:

app/adapters/local-storage.js

```
import Adapter from '@ember-data/adapter';
import { resolve, reject } from 'rsvp';
import { pluralize } from 'ember-inflector';
```

---

[1]https://github.com/tildeio/rsvp.js

```
export default class LocalStorageAdapter extends Adapter {
  _getDataFromStorage()  {
    let jsonString = localStorage.getItem(this.namespace);

    if (!jsonString) {
      return {};
    }

    return JSON.parse(jsonString);
  }

  findAll(store, type) {
    let json = this._getDataFromStorage();
    let { modelName } = type;
    let storageKeyForModelName = pluralize(modelName);
    let resources = json[storageKeyForModelName];

    if (!resources) {
      json[storageKeyForModelName] = [];
    }

    return resolve(json);
  }
}
```

To start, a "private" method called _getDataFromStorage() has been defined that reads the string of JSON from Local Storage and parses it. If there is no data, an empty object is returned. This method will be used in our other adapter methods.

Because the JSON is stored in Local Storage with the same structure as our Mirage backend, we can simply wrap it in a fulfilled promise using resolve() and return it.

Now there's one other case we need to handle, and that is to ensure findAll() still works even if Local Storage is empty. If Local Storage is empty, an empty array for the models we are trying to find is assigned to a key on json. With this, the returned promise resolves with { contacts: [] } for our application.

Visit http://localhost:4200/contacts and you should see the three contacts that were stored in Local Storage. Wasn't too bad was it? Let's move on to findRecord().

Implementing findRecord()

The general idea of findRecord() is similar to findAll(). findRecord() returns a fulfilled promise with the found resource or a rejected promise if the resource isn't found:

app/adapters/local-storage.js

```
import Adapter from '@ember-data/adapter';
import { resolve, reject } from 'rsvp';
import { pluralize } from 'ember-inflector';

export default class LocalStorageAdapter extends Adapter {
  // ...

  findRecord(store, type, id, snapshot) {
    let json = this._getDataFromStorage();
    let { modelName } = type;
    let storageKeyForModelName = pluralize(modelName);
    let resources = json[storageKeyForModelName];

    if (!resources) {
      return reject();
    }
```

```
    let foundResource = resources.find((resource) => {
      return resource.id === snapshot.id;
    });

    if (foundResource) { let payload = {};
      payload[modelName] = foundResource;
      return resolve(payload);
    }

    return reject();
  }
}
```

In the preceding implementation, `Array.prototype.find()` is used to find the first resource by `id`. If the resource is found, a fulfilled promise is returned with the resource structured just like how our API would respond to `/api/contacts/1`. For example, finding a `contact` with an `id` of 1 would result in a promise that is fulfilled with the following:

```
{
  "contact": {
    "id": 1,
    "name": "Tom",
    "phoneNumber": "(123) 456-7890"
  }
}
```

If the resource isn't found or there are no resources for that type, a rejected promise is returned using `reject()`.

Visit `http://localhost:4200/contacts/1` and you should see the edit form populated with Tom's information.

Now that `findRecord()` is complete, let's move on to `createRecord()`.

Implementing createRecord()

Instead of making a POST request via AJAX, createRecord() will instead pull all of the data out of Local Storage, push the new record to the array for the given type, and write the data back to Local Storage. When we made a POST request to our API previously, we relied on the database to return an id of the newly created record. Local Storage however doesn't have auto incrementing IDs, so we'll need to simulate that ourselves. Records will be stored in Local Storage sorted by id in ascending order. Knowing this, we can set id on a new record to the id of the last record incremented by 1. If there are no records for the given type, we can default id to the string "1". Why the string representation of a number you may ask? Ember Data coerces the id property to a string anyways behind the scenes, and our implementation becomes simpler if we stay consistent and write strings to Local Storage as well. Here is the implementation:

app/adapters/local-storage.js

```
import Adapter from '@ember-data/adapter';
import { resolve, reject } from 'rsvp';
import { pluralize } from 'ember-inflector';

export default class LocalStorageAdapter extends Adapter {
  // ...
  createRecord(store, type, snapshot) {
    let { modelName } = type;
    let data = {};
    let serializer = store.serializerFor(modelName);

    serializer.serializeIntoHash(data, type, snapshot);

    let resource = data[modelName];
    let json = this._getDataFromStorage();
    let storageKeyForModelName = pluralize(modelName);
```

```
  let resources = json[storageKeyForModelName];

  if (resources) {
    let lastResource = resources[resources.length - 1];
    resource.id = String(Number(lastResource.id) + 1);
    resources.push(resource);
  } else {
    resource.id = '1';
    json[storageKeyForModelName] = [resource];
  }

  localStorage.setItem(this.namespace, JSON.stringify(json));
  return resolve(data);
  }
}
```

Once the record has been saved, a promise that fulfills the persisted data will be returned, structured the same as how our API would respond to POST requests. For example, creating a contact named Mary would result in a promise that is fulfilled with the following:

```
{
  "contact": {
    "id": 4,
    "name": "Mary"
  }
}
```

Next up, we will tackle updateRecord().

Implementing `updateRecord()`

In our previous adapter, `updateRecord()` made a PUT request with the updated data and responded with a payload structured the same as `createRecord()`. With our Local Storage adapter, the `id` of the record will be used to find it in Local Storage. If found, the new properties will be set and the data will be written back to Local Storage. A fulfilled promise will be returned with the data. If the resource isn't found, a rejected promise will be returned:

app/adapters/local-storage.js

```
import Adapter from '@ember-data/adapter';
import { resolve, reject } from 'rsvp';
import { pluralize } from 'ember-inflector';

export default class LocalStorageAdapter extends Adapter {
  // ...
  updateRecord(store, type, snapshot) {
    let { modelName } = type;
    let data = {};
    let serializer = store.serializerFor(modelName);

    serializer.serializeIntoHash(data, type, snapshot);

    let storageKeyForModelName = pluralize(modelName);
    let json = this._getDataFromStorage();
    let resources = json[storageKeyForModelName];

    if (!resources) {
      return reject();
    }
```

```
    let resourceToUpdate = json[storageKeyForModelName].
    find((resource) => {
      return resource.id === snapshot.id;
    });

    if (resourceToUpdate) {
      let resourceUpdates = data[modelName];
      Object.assign(resourceToUpdate, resourceUpdates);
      localStorage.setItem(this.namespace, JSON.
      stringify(json));
      return resolve(data);
    }

    return reject();
  }
}
```

Similar to findRecord(), Array.prototype.find() and snapshot.id are used to find the resource to update. Remember when I said things would be simpler if we stored id as a string? snapshot.id always returns a string. If we had stored id as a number, we'd be comparing resource.id which is a number to snapshot.id which is a string, and we'd have to do some type conversion ourselves. Because we are storing id as a string, we can be sure that both resource.id and snapshot.id will be strings.

Lastly, if the resource is found, Object.assign() is used to merge all of the new properties into the resource.

Try editing a contact. Everything should work!

Implementing deleteRecord()

Rather than making a DELETE request via AJAX, deleteRecord() will
need to first find the record in Local Storage, and if found, remove it from
the array. Similar to the API that returned an empty response to a DELETE
request, we can return a promise that fulfills without any data:

app/adapters/local-storage.js

```
import Adapter from '@ember-data/adapter';
import { resolve, reject } from 'rsvp';
import { pluralize } from 'ember-inflector';

export default class LocalStorageAdapter extends Adapter {
  // ...
  deleteRecord(store, type, snapshot) {
    let json = this._getDataFromStorage();
    let { modelName } = type;
    let storageKeyForModelName = pluralize(modelName);
    let resources = json[storageKeyForModelName];

    if (!resources) {
      return reject();
    }

    let indexOfResourceToDelete = resources.
    findIndex((resource) => {
      return resource.id === snapshot.id;
    });

    if (indexOfResourceToDelete > -1) {
      resources.splice(indexOfResourceToDelete, 1);

      if (resources.length === 0) {
        delete json[storageKeyForModelName];
      }
```

```
    localStorage.setItem(this.namespace, JSON.
    stringify(json));
    return resolve();
  }

  return reject();
 }
}
```

In the preceding code, there is a check to see if any data exists in Local Storage for the given type. If not, a rejected promise is returned. Next, we try to find the index of the resource that is to be deleted using `Array.prototype. findIndex()`. If the resource is found, `indexOfResourceToDelete` will be greater than –1, which can be used in conjunction with `Array.prototype. slice()` to remove the resource from our list of resources. Once the resource has been removed, if our list of resources for the given type is empty, the key that holds our data is deleted. The JSON data is then written back to Local Storage, and a fulfilled promise is returned. Lastly, if the resource to be deleted was never found, a rejected promise is returned, similar to what would happen if a DELETE request to an endpoint like `/api/contacts/1` returned a 404.

Try out the application again, and see all of our CRUD operations are still working, but this time using Local Storage!

Summary

We saw how we can swap our backend with Local Storage by only making changes to our adapter and not the rest of our application code. Let's continue on and learn how to handle nested resource paths and relationship links in the next chapter.

CHAPTER 7

Nested Resource URL Paths and Relationship Links

Many APIs use nested resource URL paths to express relationships. An example of a nested resource URL path is `/contacts/1/pets`, where the collection of `pet` resources returned from this endpoint belongs to the `contact` resource with an `id` of 1. These endpoints are often referred to as relationship links, and Ember Data knows how to use them to load relationships. Let's look at the default behavior of how Ember Data uses relationship links in response payloads. Then, we will look at how to tell Ember Data about relationship links if they aren't present in an API.

The code for this chapter can be found in the chapter-7 folder of the source code for this book.

© David Tang 2021

D. Tang, *Pro Ember Data*, https://doi.org/10.1007/978-1-4842-6561-1_7

How Relationship Links Work

Ember Data supports relationship links out of the box for both the RESTAdapter and the JSONAPIAdapter. In this section, we will specifically look at relationship links with the RESTAdapter and RESTSerializer, but the same ideas apply when using JSON:API.

The RESTAdapter supports a property called links on individual resources, which contains URLs that point to related resources. For example, let's say we have a contact model with asynchronous belongsTo and hasMany relationships:

app/models/contact.js

```
import Model, { attr, hasMany, belongsTo } from '@ember-data/
model';

export default class ContactModel extends Model {
  @attr('string') name;
  @hasMany('pet', { async: true }) pets;
  @belongsTo('company', { async: true }) company;
}
```

If we made a request to /api/contacts and the response payload adhered to the RESTSerializer or the JSONSerializer formats, each contact resource in the response can have a links property:

```
{
  "contacts": [
    {
      "id": 1,
      "name": "David",
      "links": {
        "company": "/api/contacts/1/company",
        "pets": "/api/contacts/1/pets"
```

```
        }
      }
    ]
}
```

The `links` property can exist similarly on a single resource payload that is returned from an endpoint like /api/contacts/1:

```
{
  "contact": {
    "id": 1,
    "name": "David",
    "links": {
      "company": "/api/contacts/1/company",
      "pets": "/api/contacts/1/pets"
    }
  }
}
```

If we access `contact.pets` or `contact.company`, Ember Data will trigger a fetch using the URLs defined in `links`. As noted in the API documentation:

Note   The format of your links value will influence the final request URL via the urlPrefix method: Links beginning with //, http://, https://, will be used as is, with no further manipulation. Links beginning with a single / will have the current adapter's host value prepended to it. Links with no beginning / will have a parentURL prepended to it, via the current adapter's buildURL.

Lots of APIs offer endpoints that follow a nested resource URL path convention, but don't return them in the links property in a resource. Let's find out how we can tell Ember Data about these endpoints.

When APIs Don't Return Relationship Links

In the previous chapters, we learned about the different normalization methods in serializers that allow us to intercept a payload before Ember Data uses it. To handle the missing links property, we can override one of the many normalization methods.

For example, let's say calling store.findRecord('contact', 1) makes a request to /api/contacts/1 and returns the following payload:

```
{
  "contact": {
    "id": 1,
    "name": "David"
  }
}
```

We want to add links to this contact resource for the pet and company relationships. Although we could override a few different normalization methods, the simplest approach is to override normalize() since it operates on a single resource:

app/serializers/contact.js

```
import RESTSerializer from '@ember-data/serializer/rest';

export default class ContactSerializer extends RESTSerializer {
  normalize(modelClass, resourceHash) {
    resourceHash.links = {
      pets: '/api/contacts/${resourceHash.id}/pets',
      company: '/api/contacts/${resourceHash.id}/company'
    };
```

```
    return super.normalize(...arguments);
  }
}
```

And that's really it! Pretty simple huh?

As mentioned earlier, JSON:API uses `links` too, but the response format is a little different. If you do find yourself needing to manually add `links` when using JSON:API, the process is similar to the example in this chapter. Visit the JSON:API specification on links[1] for more details.

Summary

Now that we know how to work with relationship links, let's move on and learn about the different ways we can work with nested data.

---

[1]`https://jsonapi.org/format/#document-links`

CHAPTER 8

Working with Nested Data and Embedded Records

In this chapter, we'll look at two ways of handling nested data in API payloads. The first approach involves defining a model attribute without a transform. The second approach makes uses of embedded records. Let's dive in!

Declaring Attributes Without Transforms

Let's say we have the following JSON for a contact resource with address being a nested object:

```
{
  "id": 1,
  "name": "Richard Hendrix",
  "address": {
    "street": "123 Main St.",
    "zip": "90003"
  }
}
```

In Chapter 1 – Ember Data Overview, we learned about the four different transforms: string, number, boolean, and date. There is no object transform. In order to have an address attribute on the model that contains an object, we can declare the attribute without a transform:

app/models/contact.js

```
import Model, { attr } from '@ember-data/model';

export default class ContactModel extends Model {
  @attr('string')  name;
  @attr address;
}
```

When we don't specify a transform, Ember Data will just pass through the value and set it on the model.

To change a specific property on address, use dot notation with model.set():

```
model.set('address.street', '1234 New St.');
```

Now let's say we have the following JSON for a contact resource:

```
{
  "id": 1,
  "name": "Richard Hendricks",
  "history": [
    { "url": "http://piedpiper.com", "time":
    "2015-10-01T20:12:53Z" },
    { "url": "http://hooli.com", "time": "2014-10-01T20:12:53Z"
},
    { "url": "http://endframe.com", "time":
    "2013-10-01T20:12:53Z" }
  ]
}
```

There is a history property containing an array of URLs. We won't specify a transform on the model so the history data will be passed through and set on the record:

app/models/contact.js

```
import Model, { attr } from '@ember-data/model';

export default class ContactModel extends Model {
  @attr('string') name;
  @attr history;
}
```

Let's see how we can work with the history attribute. You might think we could modify a history item and expect the UI to update:

```
model.history[0].url = 'http://amazon.com';
```

However, this won't work. If we need to modify a specific history item, we will need to use set, for example:

```
import { set } from '@ember/object';

let googleItem = model.history[0];
set(googleItem, 'url', 'http://amazon.com');
```

Using set() will change the property and notify Ember to rerender. Alternatively, we can create a new array reference and reassign the history attribute:

```
let modifiedHistory = [...model.history, 'http://amazon.com'];
model.set('history', modifiedHistory);
```

Embedded Records

Nested objects with an id can also be treated as records using the mixin
EmbeddedRecordsMixin. Let's assume the JSON now looks like this:

```
{
  "id": 1,
  "name": "Richard Hendricks",
  "skills": [
    { "id": 1, "name": "Compression" },
    { "id": 2, "name": "Java" },
    { "id": 3, "name": "Algorithms" }
  ]
}
```

We can turn each object under skills into records with a hasMany
relationship established between contact and skill:

app/models/contact.js

```
import Model, { attr, hasMany } from '@ember-data/model';

export default class ContactModel extends Model {
  @attr('string') name;
  @hasMany('skill') skill;
}
```

To have Ember Data establish the hasMany relationship, we can use the
EmbeddedRecordsMixin in our serializer:

app/serializers/contact.js

```
import JSONSerializer from '@ember-data/serializer/json';
import { EmbeddedRecordsMixin } from '@ember-data/serializer/
rest';
```

```
export default class ContactSerializer extends JSONSerializer.
extend(
  EmbeddedRecordsMixin
) {
  attrs = {
    skills: { embedded: 'always' }
  };
}
```

In the attrs property, set skills to { embedded: 'always' }.
This also works for a belongsTo relationship. This example is using the
JSONSerializer, but the same technique can apply to an API based on the
RESTSerializer. Note that EmbeddedRecordsMixin does not work with the
JSONAPISerializer.

EmbeddedRecordsMixin also works with nested data inside of nested
data! For example, let's say each skill now has an embedded category
model:

```
{
  "id": 1,
  "name": "Richard Hendricks",
  "skills": [
    {
      "id": 1,
      "name": "Compression",
      "category": {
        "id": 3,
        "name": "Technology"
      }
    },
```

```
    {
      "id": 2,
      "name": "Algorithms",
      "category": {
        "id": 6,
        "name": "Technology"
      }
    }
  ]
}
```

Similar to the preceding code, create a category model and specify the relationship:

app/models/skill.js

```
import Model, { attr, belongsTo } from '@ember-data/model';

export default class SkillModel extends Model {
  @attr('string') name;
  @belongsTo('category', { async: false }) category;
}
```

app/models/category.js

```
import Model, { attr } from '@ember-data/model';

export default class CategoryModel extends Model {
  @attr('string') name;
}
```

Next, create a `skill` serializer that uses EmbeddedRecordsMixin:

app/serializers/skill.js

```
import RESTSerializer, {
  EmbeddedRecordsMixin
} from '@ember-data/serializer/rest';

export default class SkillSerializer extends RESTSerializer.
extend(
  EmbeddedRecordsMixin
) {
  attrs = {
    category: { embedded: 'always' }
  };
}
```

Nested models can recursively use the EmbeddedRecordsMixin to handle records nested in records.

Summary

In this chapter, we looked at a few different ways of handling nested data and embedded records. If we need nested data to be turned into a record, use the EmbeddedRecordsMixin. Otherwise, declare the attribute without a transform.

Up until now, we've looked at how to work with successful API responses. In the next chapter, we will look at how to handle error responses.

CHAPTER 9

Handling Custom Error Responses

So far we've looked at working with APIs that return success responses. In this chapter, we will look at how Ember Data handles errors out of the box and the different adapter and serializer methods we can override to handle custom error responses. Let's dive in!

Validation Errors

Responses with an HTTP status code of 422 (Unprocessable Entity) are considered invalid errors, or in other words, validation errors. Validation error responses follow the JSON:API specification regardless of which serializer is used. A JSON:API error response looks like the following:

```
{
  "errors": [
    {
      "id": "{unique identifier for this particular
      occurrence}",
      "links": {
        "about": "{link that leads to further details about
        this problem}"
      },
```

```
    "status": "{HTTP status code}",
    "code": "{application-specific error code}",
    "title": "{summary of the problem}",
    "detail": "{explanation specific to this occurrence of
    the problem}",
    "source": {
      "pointer": "{a JSON Pointer to the associated entity in
      the request document}",
      "parameter": "{a string indicating which URI query
      parameter caused the error}"
    },
    "meta": {}
  }
 ]
}
```

The response must contain a root key errors that is an array of error objects. Each error object can have any of the properties listed earlier. To find out more about each property of an error object, visit the JSON:API error documentation.[1] JSON:API states that an error object *may* have those properties, but Ember Data only requires a subset of them.

Let's say we want to create a new contact record and handle the scenario when there is an error validating the name attribute. The error response needs two properties: detail and source:

```
{
  "errors": [
    {
      "detail": "Name must be at least 2 characters.",
      "source": {
```

```
      "pointer": "data/attributes/name"
    }
  }
 ]
}
```

The value of source.pointer in an error object is a *JSON Pointer*[2] to a specific attribute, which in this case is the name attribute. A JSON Pointer is a string using a syntax that is similar to a file path, where it identifies a path to a specific value in a JSON document.

When the adapter sees a 422 response status code, a rejected promise is returned with an instance of InvalidError to signal that the record failed server-side validation. The InvalidError instance is passed errors from the response payload. These validation errors can then be retrieved from the record with the errors property. For example, we can render the record's validation errors for the name attribute as follows:

```
{{#each model.errors.name as |error|}}
  <div class="error">
    {{error.message}}
  </div>
{{/each}}
```

We can also access these errors and the instance of InvalidError in our catch block:

```
try {
  await contact.save();
} catch (invalidError) {
  console.log(invalidError); // instance of InvalidError
  console.log(contact.errors); // instance of Errors
```

---

[2]JSON Pointer defines a string syntax for identifying a specific value within a JavaScript Object Notation (JSON) document.

```
console.log(contact.get('errors.name'));
// array of error objects for the name attribute
console.log(contact.isValid); // false
}
```

Controlling the Invalid Status Code

Your first question might be "What if my API returns a status code other than 422?" If we look at the RESTAdapter source code, we can see the creation of InvalidError only happens if the status is invalid via the isInvalid() method:

```
isInvalid(status, headers, payload) {
  return status === 422;
},

handleResponse(status, headers, payload, requestData) {
  if (this.isSuccess(status, headers, payload)) {
    return payload;
  } else if (this.isInvalid(status, headers, payload)) {
    return new InvalidError(payload.errors);
  }
  // ...
  return new AdapterError(errors, detailedMessage);
}
```

We can override the public isInvalid() method in our adapter to account for a status code that isn't 422. For example, maybe our API responds with 400 instead of 422:

app/adapters/application.js

```
import RESTAdapter from '@ember-data/adapter/rest';

export default class ApplicationAdapter extends RESTAdapter {
  namespace = 'api';
```

```
  isInvalid(status) {
    return status === 400;
  }
}
```

Controlling Error Response Payloads

Your second question might be "What if my error response payload doesn't follow JSON:API?"

Let's say our error response looks like the following instead:

```
{
  "errors": {
    "name": "Name must be at least 2 characters."
  }
}
```

If the payload contains an errors property that isn't an array, you will get the following error message in the console:

Error   AdapterError expects json-api formatted errors array.

The reason this error message mentions AdapterError instead of InvalidError is because InvalidError extends from the AdapterError class.

Let's look at the implementation of handleResponse() again:

```
handleResponse(status, headers, payload, requestData) {
  if (this.isSuccess(status, headers, payload)) {
    return payload;
  } else if (this.isInvalid(status, headers, payload)) {
    return  new InvalidError(payload.errors);
  }
```

105

```
// ...
  return new AdapterError(errors, detailedMessage);
}
```

As you can see, the errors property of the payload is passed directly to
InvalidError, and if it isn't an array, the preceding error message will be
thrown. To handle a custom error payload that either doesn't have errors
as an array or doesn't have an errors property at all, we can override
handleResponse() in the adapter:

app/adapters/application.js

```
import RESTAdapter from 'ember-data/adapters/rest';

export default class ApplicationAdapter extends RESTAdapter {
  namespace = 'api';

  handleResponse(status, headers, payload, requestData) {
    if (this.isInvalid(status)) {
      payload.errors = Object.keys(payload.errors).
      map((attribute) => {
        return {
          detail: payload.errors[attribute],
          source: {
            pointer: 'data/attributes/${attribute}'
          }
        };
      });
    }

    return super.handleResponse(status, headers, payload,
    requestData);
  }
}
```

In the preceding code, we are manipulating our custom error payload to be JSON:API compliant if the status is invalid. Then, the original handleResponse() is called so that the InvalidError object is created.

Now your third question might be "What if the payload does have an errors property that is an array, but it isn't JSON:API compliant?" Let's say our error payload looked like this instead:

```
{
  "errors": [
    {
      "attribute": "name",
      "messages": {
        "size": "Name must be at least 2 characters.",
        "alpha": "Name must be entirely alphabetic characters."
      }
    }
  ]
}
```

Each of the validation rules and corresponding messages are stored under errors/messages. To handle this error payload, we can override handleResponse() as before, or we can override the extractErrors() method on the serializer. The extractErrors() method is used to extract model errors when a call to save() on the model fails with an InvalidError. The extractErrors() method receives the payload as one of its arguments and expects the return value to look like the following:

```
{
  name: [
    'Name must be at least 2 characters.',
    'Name must be entirely alphabetic characters.'
  ];
}
```

Here is an implementation of overriding extractErrors() to normalize the errors array in the response:

app/serializers/contact.js

```
import ApplicationSerializer from './application';

export default class ContactSerializer extends
ApplicationSerializer {
  extractErrors(store, typeClass, payload, id) {
    let extractedErrors = {};

    payload.errors.forEach((error) => {
      extractedErrors[error.attribute] = Object.keys(error.
      messages).map(
        (rule) => {
          return error.messages[rule];
        }
      );
    });

    return extractedErrors;
  }
}
```

So your fourth question might be "Why bother using extractErrors() if I could just use handleResponse() for all cases?" The answer to that goes back to the question "what class is responsible for formatting request and response data?" That's the serializer. Generally, if I can handle normalizing error responses in the serializer, I prefer that. If normalization isn't possible in the serializer, then I will handle it in the adapter.

Other Error Types

We learned about the InvalidError class that gets instantiated when there is a 422 response. Ember Data also supports a few other error types for common HTTP status codes (Table 9-1).

Table 9-1. *Common HTTP Status Codes*

Error Class	HTTP Status Code
InvalidError	422
UnauthorizedError	401
ForbiddenError	403
NotFoundError	404
ConflictError	409
ServerError	500

An UnauthorizedError will get thrown if the HTTP status code is 401, which indicates that authorization is required and has either failed or not been provided. A ForbiddenError will get thrown if the HTTP status code is 403, which signals that the authenticated user doesn't have the necessary permissions for the request. A NotFoundError will get thrown if the HTTP status code is 404, which indicates that the server can't find a resource. A ConflictError will get thrown if the HTTP status code is 409, which indicates that there is a request conflict with the state of the server. For example, a 409 status could be returned if a user was trying to update a resource with stale data. Lastly, a ServerError will get thrown if the HTTP status code is 500, which indicates that there was an error on the server.

All of these error classes also extend from the AdapterError class.

Let's say our API returns a 500 status code. When this happens, the following will hold true:

```
import AdapterError, {
  ServerError,
  TimeoutError
} from '@ember-data/adapter/error';

// ...

try {
  await contact.save();
} catch (serverError) {
  console.log(serverError instanceof AdapterError); // true
  console.log(serverError instanceof ServerError); // true
  console.log(serverError instanceof TimeoutError); // false
}
```

As we learned with InvalidError, the expected error payload needs to have an errors property as an array. This is true for any subclass of AdapterError.

Let's say our API responds with a 500 status code and the following payload:

```
{
  "errors": [
    {
      "status": "500",
      "title": "There was an error on the server.",
      "detail": "Oh snap! Something went wrong.",
      "foo": "bar"
    },
```

```
    {
      "bar": "baz"
    }
  ]
}
```

With this payload, the errors property on our ServerError instance will be this:

```
[
  {
    status: '500',
    title: 'There was an error on the server.',
    detail: 'Oh snap! Something went wrong.',
    foo: 'bar'
  },
  {
    bar: 'baz'
  }
];
```

If an errors key isn't present in the response, the adapter will create the following for errors on our ServerError instance:

```
[
  {
    status: '500',
    title: 'The backend responded with an error',
    // this message is created by Ember Data
    detail: '[object Object]' // A string representation of
                                           the payload
  }
];
```

If the API returns a string as a payload, such as "FAILED", detail will be that string:

```
[
  {
    status: '500',
    title: 'The backend responded with an error',
    // this message is created by Ember Data
    detail: 'FAILED'
  }
];
```

Personally, I haven't found the need to normalize error payloads that weren't validation errors (InvalidError), but if you need to, you can override handleResponse() in the adapter like we did earlier. For example, let's say the API returned a 500 with the following response:

```
{
  "status": "500",
  "title": "There was an error on the server.",
  "detail": "Oh snap! Something went wrong.",
  "foo": "bar"
}
```

In this case, errors on our ServerError instance would contain the following:

```
[
  {
    status: '500',
    title: 'The backend responded with an error',
    // this message is created by Ember Data
    detail: '[object Object]' // A string representation of
                                        the payload
  }
];
```

We could normalize this error response in handleResponse() as follows:

```
import RESTAdapter from '@ember-data/adapter/rest';

export default class ApplicationAdapter extends RESTAdapter {
  handleResponse(status, headers, payload, requestData) {
    if (status === 500) {
      let normalizedPayload = {
        errors: [payload]
      };

      return super.handleResponse(
        status,
        headers,
        normalizedPayload,
        requestData
      );
    }

    return super.handleResponse(status, headers, payload,
    requestData);
  }
}
```

Here we are taking the raw payload and putting it in an errors array in an object. With this change, errors on our ServerError instance would contain the following:

```
[
  {
    status: '500',
    title: 'There was an error on the server.',
    detail: 'Oh snap! Something went wrong.',
    foo: 'bar'
  }
];
```

Summary

Handling errors is an important aspect when working with APIs, and Ember Data is flexible enough to handle any error response. In this chapter, we looked at the default error handling in Ember Data and learned about validation errors and other adapter errors. Next up, we'll learn about different ways of testing our Ember Data customizations.

CHAPTER 10

Testing Adapters and Serializers

In this chapter, we'll look at how to test adapters and serializers.

Testing Adapters

Whenever we generate an adapter, a corresponding unit test is generated. Here is the default test:

tests/unit/adapters/application-test.js

```js
import { module, test } from 'qunit';
import { setupTest } from 'ember-qunit';

module('Unit | Adapter | application', function (hooks) {
  setupTest(hooks);

  // Replace this with your real tests.
  test('it exists', function (assert) {
    let adapter = this.owner.lookup('adapter:application');
    assert.ok(adapter);
  });
});
```

Adapters are quite easy to test. We can get access to an adapter instance by looking it up in the container with `this.owner.lookup()`. Then we can call any of our overridden methods.

In Chapter 9 – Handling Custom Error Responses, we learned that responses with a 422 status code are treated as server-side validation errors. What if instead we want all responses with a 400 or 422 status code to be treated as validation errors? As we did in the last chapter, we can override the `isInvalid()` method:

app/adapters/application.js

```
import RESTAdapter from '@ember-data/adapter/rest';

export default class ApplicationAdapter extends RESTAdapter {
  isInvalid(status) {
    return status === 400 || status === 422;
  }
}
```

To test this, we can invoke `isInvalid()` with the 400 and 422 status codes and assert the return value is `true`. We can also invoke it with a status code that is neither 400 nor 422 and assert the return value is `false`:

tests/unit/adapters/application-test.js

```
import { module, test } from 'qunit';
import { setupTest } from 'ember-qunit';

module('Unit | Adapter | application', function (hooks) {
  setupTest(hooks);
  test('isInvalid() returns true for a 400 status code',
  function (assert) {
    let adapter = this.owner.lookup('adapter:application');
    assert.ok(adapter.isInvalid(400));
  });
```

```
test('isInvalid() returns true for a 422 status code',
function (assert) {
  let adapter = this.owner.lookup('adapter:application');
  assert.ok(adapter.isInvalid(422));
});

test('isInvalid() returns false for a 500 status code',
function (assert) {
  let adapter = this.owner.lookup('adapter:application');
  assert.notOk(adapter.isInvalid(500));
  });
});
```

That's really it when it comes to unit testing adapters. Later on in this chapter, we'll look at how we can test an adapter and serializer together.

Testing Serializers

Every time a serializer is generated, a corresponding unit test file is also generated with two tests. If you don't already have a unit test for the application serializer, go ahead and create one:

```
ember generate serializer-test application
```

You should see the following contents in tests/unit/serializers/application-test.js:

tests/unit/serializers/application-test.js

```
import { module, test } from 'qunit';
import { setupTest } from 'ember-qunit';

module('Unit | Serializer | application', function (hooks) {
  setupTest(hooks);
```

```
// Replace this with your real tests.
test('it exists', function (assert) {
  let store = this.owner.lookup('service:store');
  let serializer = store.serializerFor('application');

  assert.ok(serializer);
});

test('it serializes records', function (assert) {
  let store = this.owner.lookup('service:store');
  let record = store.createRecord('application', {});

  let serializedRecord = record.serialize();

  assert.ok(serializedRecord);
});
});
```

The first test shows an example serializer test where we can test a serializer directly by getting an instance of the serializer through the store, invoking methods on it, and writing assertions against those results. The second test shows an example where we might want to test serialization logic through a record. Given that the application serializer isn't tied to a specific model (i.e., there is no application model), we can delete that second test.

Now, let's write a few application serializer tests to verify that payloads are being normalized and serialized correctly. Let's assume our API follows the RESTSerializer format and that all of the keys in the payload are snake_cased. For example, GET /api/contacts might return the following:

```
{
  "contacts": [
    { "id": 1, "first_name": "Tom" },
    { "id": 2, "first_name": "Yehuda" }
  ]
}
```

Let's write a test to verify that a snake_cased key like `first_name` maps to a camelCased attribute on our model like `firstName`. The `keyForAttribute()` method can be used to define rules for how to convert an attribute name in a model to a key in a JSON payload:

tests/unit/serializers/application-test.js

```
import { module, test } from 'qunit';
import { setupTest } from 'ember-qunit';

module('Unit | Serializer | application', function (hooks) {
  setupTest(hooks);

  test('snake_cased JSON attribute keys map to camelCased model
  attributes', function (assert) {
    let store = this.owner.lookup('service:store');
    let serializer = store.serializerFor('application');

    assert.equal(serializer.keyForAttribute('firstName'),
    'first_name');
  });
});
```

Our test should be failing. To get this test passing, let's implement `keyForAttribute()` in our application serializer:

app/serializers/application.js

```
import RESTSerializer from '@ember-data/serializer/rest';
import { underscore } from '@ember/string';
```

```
export default class ApplicationSerializer extends
RESTSerializer {
  keyForAttribute(attr) {
    return underscore(attr);
  }
}
```

Success! Our test is now passing.

In our application, let's say we update a `contact` record somewhere with the following code:

```
contact.firstName = firstName;
contact.save();
```

The root key of the outgoing PUT `/contacts/:id` request will be this:

```
{
  "contact": {
    "first_name": "David"
  }
}
```

If we want the root key for all outgoing requests to be plural, we can override the `payloadKeyFromModelName()` method. Let's write a test first:

tests/unit/serializers/application-test.js

```
import { module, test } from 'qunit';
import { setupTest } from 'ember-qunit';

module('Unit | Serializer | application', function (hooks) {
  setupTest(hooks);

  test('snake_cased JSON attribute keys map to camelCased model
  attributes', function (assert) {
    // ...
  });
```

```
test('the root key for all outgoing requests is plural',
function (assert) {
  let store = this.owner.lookup('service:store');
  let serializer = store.serializerFor('application');
  let type = serializer.payloadKeyFromModelName('contact');
  assert.equal(type, 'contacts');
});
});
```

And here is the implementation to get that test passing:

app/serializers/application.js

```
import RESTSerializer from '@ember-data/serializer/rest';
import { underscore } from '@ember/string';
import { pluralize } from 'ember-inflector';

export default class ApplicationSerializer extends
RESTSerializer {
  // ...

  payloadKeyFromModelName(modelName) {
    let rootKey = super.payloadKeyFromModelName(modelName);
    return pluralize(rootKey);
  }
}
```

I have found that testing a serializer by calling methods on an instance of a serializer as shown in this section can be useful when testing generic customizations that will apply to several models, like the application serializer. If the customizations are very simple like the ones mentioned earlier, my acceptance tests can often times cover these cases and I don't need to have dedicated serializer tests. In any case, now you know how to unit test a serializer if you need to.

Testing Adapters and Serializers Together

Typically, we don't write code that interacts with adapters and serializers directly. We use adapters and serializers indirectly through the store. In some cases, we may want to write a higher-level test that verifies all of our adapter and serializer customizations are working together correctly. In these cases, it can be helpful to write a test where we utilize the store, similar to how we would use the store in our application. Let's look at a few examples.

Testing Normalization

In earlier chapters, we learned about the `normalizeResponse()` method, which is used to normalize a payload from the server to a JSON:API document. Let's look at how we can test a normalization method using the store. Let's say we have a GET `/api/contacts` API endpoint that returns the following JSON:

```
{
  "data": [
    { "id": 1, "name": "Tom Dale" },
    { "id": 2, "name": "Yehuda Katz" }
  ]
}
```

We want to extract out that `data` key, just like we did in Chapter 4 – Common Adapter and Serializer Customizations, so that when we call `store.findAll()`, Ember Data can correctly normalize the list of contacts found under the `data` key. Let's start with our test:

tests/unit/serializers/contact.js

```
import { module, test } from 'qunit';
import { setupTest } from 'ember-qunit';
```

```
import { setupMirage } from 'ember-cli-mirage/test-support';
import { Response } from 'miragejs';

module('Unit | Serializer | contact', function (hooks) {
  setupTest(hooks);
  setupMirage(hooks);

  test('normalizing findAll()', async function (assert) {
    this.server.get('/api/contacts', function () {
      return new Response(
        200,
        {},
        {
          data: [
            { id: 1, name: 'Fiona' },
            { id: 2, name: 'Steve' }
          ]
        }
      );
    });

    let store = this.owner.lookup('service:store');
    let contacts = await store.findAll('contact');
    assert.equal(contacts.length, 2);
  });
});
```

This test uses Ember CLI Mirage[1] to mock out the API. For the GET /
api/contacts endpoint, we specified a static response in the same format
that the API is expected to return. Next, we can access the store from the
container and call findAll(). When the promise resolves, an assertion

---

[1] www.ember-cli-mirage.com/

is made to verify that the RecordArray length equals how many contacts were under the data key in the response.

Now let's write our implementation to get this test passing. First, let's make sure our adapter has the api namespace:

app/adapters/application.js

```
import RESTAdapter from '@ember-data/adapter/rest';

export default class ApplicationAdapter extends RESTAdapter {
  namespace = 'api';
}
```

Second, here is the implementation of our serializer, which we saw earlier in Chapter 4 – Common Adapter and Serializer Customizations:

app/serializers/contact.js

```
import JSONSerializer from '@ember-data/serializer/json';

export default class ContactSerializer extends JSONSerializer {
  normalizeResponse(store, primaryModelClass, payload, id,
  requestType) {
    return super.normalizeResponse(
      store,
      primaryModelClass,
      payload.data,
      id,
      requestType
    );
  }
}
```

With this implementation, our test is passing.

I tend to prefer testing adapter and serializer customizations this way for a few reasons. First, the code in the test is similar to the majority of code that I would write in my application. My application invokes methods on the store, not on adapters and serializers. I have found that this approach often times makes my tests easier to understand. Second, this test triggered both our adapter and serializer together. Third, this type of test creates a lot more flexibility when it comes to refactoring. For example, let's say later on I decide that I only want this normalization to happen when we are expecting an array to come back such as when calling store.findAll() or store.query(). In this case, I would want to override normalizeArrayResponse() instead, as we learned in Chapter 5 – Writing an Adapter and Serializer from Scratch. The updated serializer implementation would look like this:

app/serializers/contact.js

```
import JSONSerializer from '@ember-data/serializer/json';

export default class ContactSerializer extends JSONSerializer {
  normalizeArrayResponse(store, primaryModelClass, payload, id,
  requestType) {
    return super.normalizeArrayResponse(
      store,
      primaryModelClass,
      payload.data,
      id,
      requestType
    );
  }
}
```

Even though I changed the normalization implementation, my test did not need to change.

Testing Serialization

Now let's test that our serializer can serialize data correctly when creating and updating resources. When we create a new contact record and call save(), we want to verify that the request payload is formatted the way the API expects it. Imagine the API expects the request payload for POST /api/contacts to look like the following:

```
{
  "data": {
    "firstName": "Zoey"
  }
}
```

Let's also assume the response payload for POST /api/contacts looks like the following:

```
{
  "data": {
    "id": "1",
    "firstName": "Zoey"
  }
}
```

Continuing from the previous example where our contact serializer was extending JSONSerializer, the default request payload that will get sent to the API looks like this:

```
{
  "firstName": "Zoey"
}
```

The default response payload would be:

```
{
  "id": "1",
  "firstName": "Zoey"
}
```

Let's write a test to capture the serialization customizations we'll need to make:

tests/unit/serializers/contact-test.js

```
import { module, test } from 'qunit';
import { setupTest } from 'ember-qunit';
import { setupMirage } from 'ember-cli-mirage/test-support';
import { Response } from 'miragejs';

module('Unit | Serializer | contact', function (hooks) {
  setupTest(hooks);
  setupMirage(hooks);

  test('normalizing findAll()', async function (assert) {
    // ...
  });

  test('serialization', async function (assert) {
    this.server.post('/api/contacts', function (schema,
    request) {
      let requestPayload = JSON.parse(request.requestBody);

      assert.deepEqual(requestPayload, {
        data: {
          firstName: 'Zoey'
        }
      });
```

```
    return new Response(
      201,
      {},
      {
        data: {
          id: '1',
          firstName: 'Zoey'
        }
      }
    );
  });

  let store = this.owner.lookup('service:store');

  let contact = store.createRecord('contact', {
    firstName: 'Zoey'
  });

  await contact.save();
  assert.equal(contact.id, '1');
  });
});
```

In the preceding test, we are mocking out the POST /api/contacts
endpoint, creating a contact record, and saving it. In our mocked Mirage
route handler, we are writing an assertion against the request payload.
Each request object has a requestBody property, which contains the
request payload as a JSON string. With that, we can check to make sure
that the data was "sent across" correctly. Finally, we return the expected
response. This test also asserts that the id returned from the server was set
on our contact record, which verifies that the response was normalized
correctly.

In order to get our test to pass, we need to make two serializer customizations. First, we need to make sure our request payload has a data root key. As we learned in Chapter 5 – Writing an Adapter and Serializer from Scratch, we can override the serializeIntoHash() method to control the root key. Second, we need to normalize the response and extract the root data key from the payload so that Ember Data can use the resource object and assign the id to the contact record. We can override the normalizeCreateRecordResponse() for this. Here is the implementation for both customizations:

app/serializers/contact.js

```
import JSONSerializer from '@ember-data/serializer/json';

export default class ContactSerializer extends JSONSerializer {
  serializeIntoHash(hash, type, snapshot, options) {
    hash.data = this.serialize(snapshot, options);
  }

  normalizeCreateRecordResponse(
    store,
    primaryModelClass,
    payload,
    id,
    requestType
  ) {
    return super.normalizeCreateRecordResponse(
      store,
      primaryModelClass,
      payload.data,
      id,
      requestType
    );
  }
}
```

And our test is passing!

There is still room for improvement though. Looking at our test, we have one assertion at the top and another at the bottom of the test. Personally, I tend to prefer when my tests follow the Arrange-Act-Assert (AAA) pattern. If you're not familiar with this pattern, it is a way of organizing the different sections of a test. The Arrange phase includes setting up the test, like mocking out API endpoints. The Act phase includes calling the method or function under test. In this example, the Act phase is "contact.save()". The Assert phase includes all of our assertions. Following this pattern can improve the readability of a test and results in all assertions being placed at the bottom of the test. Let's see how we can restructure our test to follow Arrange-Act-Assert.

First, install Sinon.js,[2] a library that provides spies, stubs, and mocks for JavaScript:

```
npm i sinon --save-dev
```

Next, import Sinon in the test file:

tests/unit/serializers/contact-test.js

```
import sinon from 'sinon';
```

And here is our refactored test:

```
test('serialization (with sinon)', async function (assert) {
  // Arrange
  let routeHandler = sinon.stub().returns(
    new Response(
      201,
      {},
      {
```

---

[2]https://sinonjs.org/

```
      data: {
        id: '1',
        firstName: 'Zoey'
      }
    }
  )
);

this.server.post('/api/contacts', routeHandler);

let store = this.owner.lookup('service:store');

// Act
let contact = store.createRecord('contact', {
  firstName: 'Zoey'
});

await contact.save();

// Assert
assert.equal(contact.id, '1');

let request = routeHandler.getCall(0).args[1];
let requestPayload = JSON.parse(request.requestBody);
assert.deepEqual(requestPayload, {
  data: { firstName: 'Zoey' }
});
});
```

We've modified our test to use a test stub provided by Sinon for our Mirage route handler. Test stubs are functions with pre-programmed behavior. In this example, we've created a stub, routeHandler, that returns the expected response when saving a new contact record. A stub in Sinon will collect information about how it is used, like the number of times it was invoked and the arguments and return value of each invocation. In this case, we are particularly interested in capturing the request argument that the stub was invoked with so that we can access the request payload. We can get access to that information with `routeHandler.getCall(0).args[1]`. From there, we can parse `request.requestBody` and write our assertion.

Our test is passing! We've successfully refactored our test to follow the Arrange-Act-Assert pattern so that our assertions are grouped together at the end of the test, which in my opinion makes the test easier to read.

Summary

In this chapter, we looked at how to unit test adapters and serializers and how to indirectly test adapters and serializers together through the store. Ultimately, test the way that makes the most sense to you and provides the most value for your application.

CHAPTER 11

Common Customizations with JSON:API

The goal of the JSON:API specification was to put more convention into building APIs and reduce the number of conversations (hopefully not arguments) on how responses should be formatted. One of the great things about using JSON:API is that Ember Data supports it out of the box! Despite this, even if your API follows the specification, it isn't guaranteed that it will work with Ember Data. Ember Data expects a few more conventions built on top of JSON:API, which are noted in the Recommendations[1] section of the specification. In this chapter, we'll look at a few customizations we might have to make so that we can get Ember Data working with our JSON:API API.

---

[1]https://jsonapi.org/recommendations/

© David Tang 2021
D. Tang, *Pro Ember Data*, https://doi.org/10.1007/978-1-4842-6561-1_11

Changing Attribute Casing

In Chapter 3 – API Response Formats and Serializers, we discussed in "The JSONAPISerializer" section that payload attributes should be hyphenated. However, this is not part of the JSON:API specification. This convention is merely a recommendation. As noted on the recommendations page of the JSON:API specification:

Note   Member names SHOULD contain only the characters "a-z" (U+0061 to U+007A), "0-9" (U+0030 to U+0039), and the hyphen minus (U+002D HYPHEN-MINUS, "-") as separator between multiple words.

Because it is only a recommendation, you may find yourself working with a team where they opt for snake_cased or camelCased attributes instead, as it may work better for their particular server-side technology.

To accommodate payload keys that follow a different casing, we can map attributes using the attrs object like we learned about in Chapter 4 – Common Adapter and Serializer Customizations. This works well for a few attributes, but it can get tedious if you have to do it for every attribute. Luckily, there is a better approach using the keyForAttribute() method. This method can be used to convert model attributes to payload keys. For example, let's say we have the following JSON:API-compliant response that uses snake_cased attributes for two different resource types, contacts and pets:

```
{
  "data": {
    "type": "contacts",
    "id": "1",
    "attributes": {
      "first_name": "John",
      "last_name": "Doe"
    },
```

```json
    "relationships": {
      "pets": {
        "data": [
          {
            "id": 1,
            "type": "pets"
          }
        ]
      }
    }
  },
  "included": [
    {
      "type": "pets",
      "id": "1",
      "attributes": {
        "first_name": "Fiona"
      }
    }
  ]
}
```

Our contact model looks like this:

app/models/contact.js

```javascript
import Model, { attr } from '@ember-data/model';

export default class ContactModel extends Model {
  @attr('string') firstName;
  @attr('string') lastName;
}
```

Our pet model looks like this:

app/models/pet.js

```
import Model, { attr } from '@ember-data/model';

export default class PetModel extends Model {
  @attr('string') firstName;
}
```

We can override keyForAttribute() in an application serializer that extends from JSONAPISerializer so that all of these snake_cased properties get set on our models as camelCased, for example:

app/serializers/application.js

```
import JSONAPISerializer from '@ember-data/serializer/json-api';
import { underscore } from '@ember/string';

export default class ApplicationSerializer extends
JSONAPISerializer {
  keyForAttribute(attr, method) {
    return underscore(attr);
  }
}
```

The keyForAttribute() method will get called for every resource object for each model attribute. For the preceding JSON, keyForAttribute() will get called twice for firstName and lastName for the one contact resource object and once for firstName for the one pet resource object.

What if relationship properties also follow the snake_cased convention? For example, in the following JSON:API response, we have a relationship property inside_pets:

```
{
  "data": {
    "type": "contacts",
    "id": "1",
    "attributes": {
      "first_name": "John",
      "last_name": "Doe"
    },
    "relationships": {
      "inside_pets": {
        "data": [
          {
            "id": 1,
            "type": "pets"
          }
        ]
      }
    }
  },
  "included": [
    {
      "type": "pets",
      "id": "1",
      "attributes": {
        "first_name": "Fiona"
      }
    }
  ]
}
```

On our model, we would declare insidePets as a hasMany relationship:

app/models/contact.js

```
import Model, { attr, hasMany } from '@ember-data/model';

export default class ContactModel extends Model {
  @attr('string') firstName;
  @attr('string') lastName;
  @hasMany('pet', { async: false }) insidePets;
}
```

In order for this to get set on our contact model as insidePets, we can override keyForRelationship() on our serializer:

app/serializers/application.js

```
import JSONAPISerializer from '@ember-data/serializer/json-api';
import { underscore } from '@ember/string';

export default class ApplicationSerializer extends
JSONAPISerializer {
  // ...
  keyForRelationship(key, relationship, method) {
    return underscore(key);
  }
}
```

The keyForRelationship() method behaves similarly to the keyForAttribute() method.

If you need to change attribute casing for APIs that fit one of the other serializer formats, both of these methods can be overridden just as we have done in this section.

Overriding a Resource Object's Type

As we learned in Chapter 3 – API Response Formats and Serializers, every resource object has a required type property that corresponds to the model name. Depending on the server-side technology used, the type might be automatically set based on class names in the backend. If these names don't match the Ember Data model names, then errors will occur. One way to fix this is to override one of the serializer's normalization methods that we learned about.

This works, but isn't very efficient. There is a better approach using the modelNameFromPayloadKey() method on the serializer.

Let's say we have the following JSON:API response:

```
{
  "data": {
    "type": "contactModel",
    "id": "1",
    "attributes": {
      "first-name": "John",
      "last-name": "Doe"
    }
  }
}
```

Our model is named contact. To map this resource to our contact model correctly, we can create a serializer for contact and override modelNameFromPayloadKey():

app/serializers/contact.js

```
import JSONAPISerializer from '@ember-data/serializer/json-api';

export default class ContactSerializer extends
JSONAPISerializer {
```

139

```
modelNameFromPayloadKey(key) {
    return 'contact';
  }
}
```

This is much simpler than overriding one of the normalization methods. One thing to note about this method is that it gets called for other resource objects in the response. Let's say the payload now contains relationships with sideloaded data:

```
{
  "data": {
    "type": "contactModel",
    "id": "1",
    "attributes": {
      "first-name": "John",
      "last-name": "Doe"
    },
    "relationships": {
      "company": {
        "data": {
          "id": 1,
          "type": "companyModel"
        }
      }
    }
  },
  "included": [
    {
      "type": "companyModel",
      "id": "1",
      "attributes": {
```

```
      "name": "Apple"
    }
  }
 ]
}
```

The modelNameFromPayloadKey() method in our contact serializer
will get called for companyModel as well. We can adjust our implementation
so that it accounts for when the argument key is equal to companyModel:

app/serializers/contact.js

```
import JSONAPISerializer from '@ember-data/serializer/json-api';

export default class ContactSerializer extends
JSONAPISerializer {
  modelNameFromPayloadKey(key) {
    if (key === 'companyModel') {
      return 'company';
    } else if (key === 'contactModel') {
      return 'contact';
    }

    return key;
  }
}
```

If our API followed a convention where type was always our model
name suffixed with *Model,* we could make this a bit more generic by
overriding modelNameFromPayloadKey() in an application serializer:

app/serializers/application.js

```
import JSONAPISerializer from '@ember-data/serializer/json-api';

export default class ApplicationSerializer extends
JSONAPISerializer {
```

```
modelNameFromPayloadKey(key) {
  return key.replace('Model', ");
}
}
```

If we normalized the type, we'll likely need to change it back to the original value when saving records. We can use the `payloadKeyFromModelN ame(modelName)` method to do that:

app/serializers/application.js

```
import JSONAPISerializer from '@ember-data/serializer/json-api';

export default class ApplicationSerializer extends
JSONAPISerializer {
  payloadKeyFromModelName(modelName) {
    return '${modelName}Model';
  }
}
```

If we were to save a `contact` record, `type` would be set to "contactModel" as shown in the following request payload:

```
{
  "data": {
    "type": "contactModel",
    "attributes": {
      "first-name": "John",
      "last-name": "Doe"
    }
  }
}
```

Overriding HTTP Methods

The JSON:API specification states that the PATCH method should be used when updating resources. What if an API we are working with still uses PUT? At the time of this writing, there isn't a great way to override HTTP methods.

If we look at the implementation of updatedRecord in the JSONAPIAdapter, it looks almost identical to the implementation of updateRecord in the RESTAdapter. The only thing that is different is "PUT" has been changed to "PATCH":

- updateRecord() in the RESTAdapter[2]

- updateRecord() in the JSONAPIAdapter[3]

If your API is mostly JSON:API compliant, but still expects PUT instead of PATCH, we can override the private ajax() method:

app/adapters/application.js

```
import JSONAPIAdapter from '@ember-data/adapter/json-api';

export default class ApplicationAdapter extends JSONAPIAdapter
{
  // BEWARE! This method is private!
  ajax(url, type, options) {
    if (type === 'PATCH') {
      type = 'PUT';
    }

    return super.ajax(url, type, options);
  }
}
```

---

[2]https://github.com/emberjs/data/blob/v3.21.0/packages/adapter/addon/rest.js#L763

[3]https://github.com/emberjs/data/blob/v3.21.0/packages/adapter/addon/json-api.js#L234

Just be aware that the `ajax()` method is **private**, so you may run into issues when updating Ember Data in the future.

Summary

In this chapter, we looked at a few customizations that you may need to make if you are working with a JSON:API API even though JSON:API is supported by Ember Data. From my experience, the number of customizations has been much fewer than when I have used APIs that didn't follow JSON:API at all.

CHAPTER 12

Consuming the Reddit API

In this chapter, we are going to build a simple application that consumes the Reddit API using Ember Data. As we build this, we will be making several adapter and serializer customizations and seeing them all work together. Let's get started!

Setup

I've created a simple Reddit application that displays posts from the emberjs subreddit. The code for this application can be found in the chapter-12 folder of the source code for this book.

The Reddit APIs We Will Use

We will be working with two Reddit APIs in order to create a slimmed-down version of https://www.reddit.com/r/emberjs/:

1. GET https://www.reddit.com/r/<subreddit name>.json

2. GET https://www.reddit.com/api/info.json?id=<subreddit_id>

© David Tang 2021
D. Tang, *Pro Ember Data*, https://doi.org/10.1007/978-1-4842-6561-1_12

The first API returns a list of post resources for a given subreddit name. For example, GET https://www.reddit.com/r/emberjs.json returns all posts for the emberjs subreddit. This endpoint has the same URL as the HTML page that you would normally visit but with a ".json" suffix. We will create a post model for these resources.

The second API returns a single resource containing information about a given subreddit like the title, description, URL of the page, when it was created, and how many subscribers there are. For example, GET https://www.reddit.com/api/info.json?id=t5_2tjb2 returns these details for the emberjs subreddit. We will create a subreddit model for this resource. Now you may be wondering where the value t5_2tjb2 in the id query string parameter came from. This value can be found in the response of the first API endpoint under the key subreddit_id in each post resource as you will see as follows. This key will be used to set up an asynchronous belongsTo relationship on a post record, which will be used to fetch the subreddit record.

Here are sample responses for each of these endpoints. I have removed some of the data so that it is easier to see the structure of the payloads.

Here is what the response will look like for the GET https://www.reddit.com/r/<subreddit name>.json endpoint:

```json
{
  "kind": "Listing",
  "data": {
    "children": [
      {
        "kind": "t3",
        "data": {
          "title": "Ember Data: Finding Records",
          "num_comments": 2,
```

```
          "subreddit_id": "t5_2tjb2",
          "url": "https://guides.emberjs.com/release/models/
                    finding-records/"
      },
      {
        "kind": "t3",
        "data": {
          "title": "Ember Data: Defining Models",
          "num_comments": 5,
          "subreddit_id": "t5_2tjb2",
          "url": "https://guides.emberjs.com/release/models/
                    defining-models/"
        }
      }
    ],
    "after": "t3_fuimy0",
    "before": null
  }
}
```

Here is what the the response will look like for the GET https://www.
reddit.com/api/info.json?id=<subreddit_id> endpoint:

```
{
  "kind": "Listing",
  "data": {
    "modhash":
    "aicumd7e1n985f0e542d5e66cf935817c95a95d821cfdcc56b",
    "dist": 1,
    "children": [
      {
        "kind": "t5",
```

```
      "data": {
        "display_name": "emberjs",
        "title": "ember.js: a framework for ambitious web
        developers",
        "primary_color": "#e34c32",
        "subscribers": 3867,
        "id": "2tjb2",
        "description": "Ember.js is a productive, battle-
        tested JavaScript framework for building modern web
        applications. It Includes everything you need to
        build rich UIs that work on any device.",
        "url": "/r/emberjs/",
        "created_utc": 1328907736.0
      }
    }
  ],
  "after": null,
  "before": null
 }
}
```

Now that we know what API endpoints we need to hit, let's start
building our application.

Fetching Posts in a Subreddit
The Route

Let's start off by creating a route named `reddit` that will be activated
when the user visits /:

```
ember generate route reddit --path="/"
```

148

In the route's model hook, we will query for the latest posts for the emberjs subreddit:

app/routes/reddit.js

```
import Route from '@ember/routing/route';

export default class RedditRoute extends Route {
  model() {
    return this.store.query('post', {
      subreddit: 'emberjs'
    });
  }
}
```

The Post Model

Next, let's create a post model:

```
ember generate model post title:string url:string
numComments:number
```

app/models/post.js

```
import Model, { attr } from '@ember-data/model';

export default class PostModel extends Model {
  @attr('string') title;
  @attr('string') url;
  @attr('number') numComments;
}
```

The Post and Reddit Adapters

At this point, if we look at the console, we'll see the following error:

GET http://localhost:4200/posts?subreddit=emberjs 404 (Not Found)

As we learned in previous chapters, the adapter is responsible for determining the URL of the API. Let's look at the two APIs we will be working with again:

1. GET https://www.reddit.com/r/<subreddit name>.json

2. GET https://www.reddit.com/api/info.json?id=<subreddit_id>

Both of these API endpoints have the same host of https://www.reddit.com but different URL paths. The approach we will take is creating two adapters. We'll have a reddit adapter that sets the host and could potentially handle other commonalities among Reddit API endpoints. Then we will have a post adapter that deals with the specifics of the first endpoint:

```
ember generate adapter reddit
ember generate adapter post
```

app/adapters/reddit.js

```
import RESTAdapter from '@ember-data/adapter/rest';

export default class RedditAdapter extends RESTAdapter {
  host = 'https://www.reddit.com';
}
```

app/adapters/post.js

```
import RedditAdapter from './reddit';

export default class PostAdapter extends RedditAdapter {
  namespace = 'r';
}
```

At this point, there is an error in the console because our application is making a GET request to https://www.reddit.com/r/posts?subreddit=emberjs, which isn't the correct URL. However, this URL is what we should expect when we call store.query('post', { subreddit: 'emberjs' }). The URL we want to hit is https://www.reddit.com/r/emberjs.json. Let's override urlForQuery(query) so that the application hits the correct endpoint:

app/adapters/post.js

```
import RedditAdapter from './reddit';

export default class PostAdapter extends RedditAdapter {
  namespace = 'r';

  urlForQuery(query) {
    let { subreddit } = query;
    delete query.subreddit;
    return `${this.host}/${this.namespace}/${subreddit}.json`;
  }
}
```

We are now making a request to the correct URL!

The Post Serializer

We're still getting an error in our console though:

Error   while processing route: reddit Assertion Failed: The response to `store.query` is expected to be an array but it was a single record. Please wrap your response in an array or use `store.queryRecord` to query for a single record.

The reason for this error is because Ember Data uses the `JSONAPISerializer` by default if one isn't defined. Because these APIs don't follow JSON:API, we don't want this behavior. Instead, we can extend from either the `JSONSerializer` or `RESTSerializer`. Because this API doesn't have any sideloaded resources, let's create a serializer for our post model and extend from the `JSONSerializer`:

```
ember generate serializer post
```

app/serializers/post.js

```
import JSONSerializer from '@ember-data/serializer/json';

export default class PostSerializer extends JSONSerializer {}
```

Let's look at the response again:

```
{
  "kind": "Listing",
  "data": {
    "children": [
      {
        "kind": "t3",
        "data": {
          "title": "Ember Data: Finding Records",
          "num_comments": 2,
```

```
      "subreddit_id": "t5_2tjb2",
      "url": "https://guides.emberjs.com/release/models/
      finding-records/"
    },
    {
      "kind": "t3",
      "data": {
        "title": "Ember Data: Defining Models",
        "num_comments": 5,
        "subreddit_id": "t5_2tjb2",
        "url": "https://guides.emberjs.com/release/models/
        defining-models/"
      }
    }
  ],
  "after": "t3_fuimy0",
  "before": null
  }
}
```

Because we are calling store.query(), the JSONSerializer expects the
response to contain an array. This response has an array of resources located in
data.children, which we can extract out using normalizeArrayResponse().
Now if we look at each resource, there is an extra data property. We'll want to
extract that as well, which we can do using normalize(). Ultimately, we want the
normalized payload to look like the following:

```
[
  {
    "title": "Ember Data: Finding Records",
    "num_comments": 2,
    "subreddit_id": "t5_2tjb2",
    "url": "https://guides.emberjs.com/release/models/finding-
    records/"
  },
```

```json
  {
    "title": "Ember Data: Defining Models",
    "num_comments": 5,
    "subreddit_id": "t5_2tjb2",
    "url": "https://guides.emberjs.com/release/models/defining-
    models/"
  }
]
```

Once we normalize the response to this, our post serializer will be happy. Let's go ahead and implement that:

app/serializers/post.js

```javascript
import JSONSerializer from '@ember-data/serializer/json';

export default class PostSerializer extends JSONSerializer {
  normalizeArrayResponse(store, primaryModelClass, payload, id,
  requestType) {
    return super.normalizeArrayResponse(
      store,
      primaryModelClass,
      payload.data.children,
      id,
      requestType
    );
  }

  normalize(typeClass, hash) {
    return super.normalize(typeClass, hash.data);
  }
}
```

Rendering Posts

Now that there are no more errors, let's update our template and render the data:

```
{{!-- app/templates/reddit.hbs --}}
<ul>
  {{#each @model as |post|}}
    <li>
      <a href={{post.url}} target="_blank" rel="noopener
      noreferrer">
        {{post.title}} ({{post.numComments}} comments)
      </a>
    </li>
  {{/each}}
</ul>
```

Fixing the Post Serializer

If we look at the page, we'll notice that the post's url and title are rendering, but not numComments. If we open up the Data tab in the Ember Inspector and view a post record, we can see that numComments is undefined. As we learned in Chapter 3 – API Response Formats and Serializers, the JSON keys when using the JSONSerializer are expected to be camelCased by default. Let's update our post serializer to handle snake_cased keys by overriding keyForAttribute():

app/serializers/post.js

```
import JSONSerializer from '@ember-data/serializer/json';
import { underscore } from '@ember/string';

export default class PostSerializer extends JSONSerializer {
  keyForAttribute(attr) {
```

```
    return underscore(attr);
  }

  normalizeArrayResponse(store, primaryModelClass, payload, id,
  requestType) {
    return super.normalizeArrayResponse(
      store,
      primaryModelClass,
      payload.data.children,
      id,
      requestType
    );
  }

  normalize(typeClass, hash) {
    return super.normalize(typeClass, hash.data);
  }
}
```

And with that, all of the data from the API is getting normalized correctly and our page is rendering as we expect! Now let's move on and fetch and display the emberjs subreddit details.

Fetching a Subreddit's Details

At the top of the page, we want to display details about the emberjs subreddit, which we can get from the second API endpoint, GET https://www.reddit.com/api/info.json?id=<subreddit_id>. As mentioned earlier, the value of subreddit_id can be obtained from subreddit_id in the first API call in each post resource.

The Subreddit Model

To start, let's create another model called `subreddit`:

```
ember generate model subreddit title:string description:string
subscribers:number
```

app/models/subreddit.js

```
import Model, { attr } from '@ember-data/model';

export default class SubredditModel extends Model {
  @attr('string') title;
  @attr('string') description;
  @attr('number') subscribers;
}
```

Next, we'll create a `belongsTo` relationship on our `post` model called `subreddit`, which will be used to asynchronously load the `subreddit` resource using the `subreddit_id` field:

app/models/post.js

```
import Model, { attr, belongsTo } from '@ember-data/model';

export default class PostModel extends Model {
  @attr('string') title;
  @attr('string') url;
  @attr('number') numComments;
  @belongsTo('subreddit', { async: true }) subreddit;
}
```

Updating the Post Serializer

If you remember from Chapter 4 – Common Adapter and Serializer Customizations, section "Mapping Foreign Keys to Relationships," in order for our subreddit relationship to be established by the JSONSerializer, we need to map subreddit_id in the API response to subreddit. We can do that using attrs, which allows us to map JSON keys in the API to attributes or relationships on our model:

app/serializers/post.js

```
import JSONSerializer from '@ember-data/serializer/json';
import { underscore } from '@ember/string';

export default class PostSerializer extends JSONSerializer {
  attrs = {
    subreddit: 'subreddit_id'
  };

  // ...
}
```

Loading the Asynchronous Subreddit Relationship

We've made this relationship asynchronous so that we can let Ember Data load the subreddit record when we access it in our template:

```
{{!-- app/templates/reddit.hbs --}}
{{#let @model.firstObject.subreddit as |subreddit|}}
  <h1>{{subreddit.title}}</h1>
  <p>{{subreddit.description}}</p>
  <p>Members: {{subreddit.subscribers}}</p>
{{/let}}
<ul>
  {{!-- ... --}}
</ul>
```

Because the subreddit record is the same for all posts, we can access any of them. In the preceding template, we are accessing the subreddit record off of the first post record.

If we open up the console, we'll see an error:

```
GET http://localhost:4200/subreddits/t5_2tjb2 404 (Not Found)
```

This isn't the correct URL that we want our application making a request to in order to load the subreddit record. If we look closely, this URL is using the correct subreddit ID and the URL looks like what we'd expect if we were to call store.findRecord('subreddit', 't5_2tjb2'). This gives us a clue as to which adapter method we'll need to override. Let's create an adapter for our subreddit model, which will also extend from our RedditAdapter, set the namespace, and override urlForFindRecord():

```
ember generate adapter subreddit
```

app/adapters/subreddit.js

```
import RedditAdapter from './reddit';

export default class SubredditAdapter extends RedditAdapter {
  namespace = 'api';

  urlForFindRecord(id) {
    return `${this.host}/${this.namespace}/info.json?id=${id}`;
  }
}
```

Our adapter is now making the correct request to https://www.reddit.com/api/info.json?id=t5_2tjb2! We're still getting a few warnings though.

Warning   Encountered "kind" in payload, but no model was found for model name "kind" (resolved model name using `DS. RESTSerializer.modelNameFromPayloadKey("kind")`).

Encountered "data" in payload, but no model was found for model name "datum" (resolved model name using `DS.RESTSerializer. modelNameFromPayloadKey("data")`).

As these pertain to the serializer, this should be a clue that we need to create a `subreddit` serializer:

```
ember generate serializer subreddit
```

app/serializers/subreddit.js

```
import JSONSerializer from '@ember-data/serializer/json';

export default class SubredditSerializer extends JSONSerializer
{}
```

We now need to normalize the `findRecord()` response, similar to what we did with our `post` serializer. Let's look at that response again:

```
{
  "kind": "Listing",
  "data": {
    "modhash":
    "aicumd7e1n985f0e542d5e66cf935817c95a95d821cfdcc56b",
    "dist": 1,
    "children": [
      {
        "kind": "t5",
        "data": {
```

```
      "display_name": "emberjs",
      "title": "ember.js: a framework for ambitious web
      developers",
      "primary_color": "#e34c32",
      "subscribers": 3867,
      "id": "2tjb2",
      "description": "Ember.js is a productive, battle-
      tested JavaScript framework for building modern web
      applications. It Includes everything you need to
      build rich UIs that work on any device.",
      "url": "/r/emberjs/",
      "created_utc": 1328907736.0
        }
      }
    ],
    "after": null,
    "before": null
  }
}
```

The subreddit resource looks like it is contained in
data.children[0].data, which we can extract out in
normalizeFindRecordResponse():

app/serializers/subreddit.js

```
import JSONSerializer from '@ember-data/serializer/json';

export default class SubredditSerializer extends JSONSerializer
{
  normalizeFindRecordResponse(
    store,
    primaryModelClass,
    payload,
```

```
    id,
    requestType
  ) {
    return super.normalizeFindRecordResponse(
      store,
      primaryModelClass,
      payload.data.children[0].data,
      id,
      requestType
    );
  }
}
```

All of the emberjs subreddit details are rendering!

Fixing the Warning Messages

We're almost done! If we open up our console, we'll see the following
warning:

Warning   You requested a record of type "subreddit" with id
"t5_2tjb2" but the adapter returned a payload with primary data
having an id of "2tjb2".

Use store.findRecord() when the requested id is the same
as the one returned by the adapter. In other cases, use "store.
queryRecord()" instead.

It looks like the response comes back with an id of 2tjb2 instead of
t5_2tjb2. Let's fix that by updating the id in the resource with the id that
we requested:

app/serializers/subreddit.js

```
import JSONSerializer from '@ember-data/serializer/json';

export default class SubredditSerializer extends JSONSerializer
{
  normalizeFindRecordResponse(
    store,
    primaryModelClass,
    payload,
    id,
    requestType
  ) {
    let resource = payload.data.children[0].data;
    resource.id = id;

    return super.normalizeFindRecordResponse(
      store,
      primaryModelClass,
      resource,
      id,
      requestType
    );
  }
}
```

Updating the id was a breeze because
normalizeFindRecordResponse() provides it as a parameter.

And with that, our application is working without any errors or
warnings!

Summary

In this chapter, we consumed two Reddit APIs with Ember Data using the `RESTAdapter` and `JSONSerializer`. We were able to achieve this without writing a ton of code. We customized several adapter and serializer properties and methods and saw how they worked together to consume a non-standard API that may have looked initially daunting.

CHAPTER 13

Polymorphic Relationships

In this chapter, we will look at polymorphism and how it relates to Ember Data. If we look up the definition of polymorphism as it relates to programming, we'll see it described as "the ability of an object to take on many forms." For example, a product could come in the form of a book or a course. In an Ember application, we would have a book model and a course model that extend from a base product model. If we extend the definition of polymorphism to relationships in our Ember Data models, it means our relationships can hold objects of different types that share a common interface, like inheriting from the same product model. Let's look at the two examples we'll be covering in this chapter.

Example 1 – Purchased Products

Imagine we have a site where users can purchase different products like courses and books. We would create a course model and a book model that extend from a base product model. We would also have a user model to represent the current user. Typically with these types of sites, there is a page that lists all of the products that the authenticated user has purchased. We could express the relationship between a user and the various products that they purchased as a hasMany relationship.

© David Tang 2021
D. Tang, *Pro Ember Data*, https://doi.org/10.1007/978-1-4842-6561-1_13

Going back to the definition of polymorphism, a user's purchased products can take on multiple forms such as a course or a book. This is an example of a polymorphic hasMany relationship, because the relationship can contain records of multiple types that all inherit from a base product class.

Example 2 – Content with Comments

Let's say our application also offers content in the form of blog posts and videos. We want users to be able to comment on each of these types of content. As such, we'll have a post model and a video model that extend from a base content model. We'll also have a comment model. Posts and videos can have many comments. A comment however can belong to a single piece of content, which in our application can be a post or a video. We could express this relationship between the comment and the content as a polymorphic belongsTo relationship, because the content associated with a comment can be of different types as long as the record inherits from our base content class.

Now that we have a few conceptual examples, let's see how we can implement this data model in Ember Data.

Setup

I have created a simple application that implements the preceding examples. The code for this application can be found in the chapter-13-restserializer folder of the source code for this book. We will use this application as a way of testing our model definitions and polymorphic relationships.

Similar to previous chapters, the API is mocked using Ember CLI Mirage.[1] In this chapter, our mock API will be following the `RESTSerializer` conventions, but the patterns and techniques covered also apply to APIs that follow the `JSONSerializer` and `JSONAPISerializer` conventions with some minor differences. If you'd like to see the code for the application when using the `JSONSerializer`, take a look at the chapter-13-jsonserializer folder of the source code for this book. If you'd like to see the code for the application when using the `JSONAPISerializer`, take a look at the chapter-13-jsonapiserializer folder of the source code for this book.

Polymorphic "hasMany" Relationships

Let's start by defining the models for Example 1 which include a product model, a course model, and a book model:

app/models/product.js

```
import Model, { attr } from '@ember-data/model';

export default class ProductModel extends Model {
  @attr('string') title;
}
```

app/models/course.js

```
import ProductModel from './product';
import { attr } from '@ember-data/model';

export default class CourseModel extends ProductModel {
  @attr('string') length;
}
```

---

[1] `www.ember-cli-mirage.com/`

app/models/book.js

```
import ProductModel from './product';
import { attr } from '@ember-data/model';

export default class BookModel extends ProductModel {
  @attr('number') pages;
}
```

As mentioned earlier, our course and book models will extend from a base product model which contains functionality common among all products, like having a title attribute.

Earlier we discussed that a user can have many purchased products. We can implement this relationship as a hasMany relationship:

app/models/user.js

```
import Model, { attr, hasMany } from '@ember-data/model';

export default class UserModel extends Model {
  @hasMany('product', {
    polymorphic: true,
    async: false
  })
  purchasedProducts;
}
```

The purchasedProducts relationship is a standard hasMany relationship but with a polymorphic option. This will allow us to store records of different types as long as they extend from the product model. I have made this a synchronous relationship in the example application, but the relationship could have been asynchronous.

Next, let's look at the expected response payload if we were to fetch a user who has purchased products. Again, our mock API will be following the RESTSerializer conventions.

In our sample application, we have the following endpoint to return the current user:

mirage/config.js

```
this.get('/users/:id', function () {
  return {
    users: {
      id: '1',
      name: 'David',
      purchasedProducts: [
        { id: '5', type: 'course' },
        { id: '10', type: 'book' }
      ]
    }
  };
});
```

As we learned in Chapter 3 – API Response Formats and Serializers, when using the RESTSerializer or the JSONSerializer, hasMany relationships should be represented in API payloads as an array of IDs. In order to use polymorphic relationships, purchasedProducts must be an array of JSON:API Resource Identifier Objects, that is, objects with id and type properties. The type property corresponds to the name of an Ember Data model in either the singular or plural form, which in this case is either course or book.

With this API response, our purchasedProducts hasMany relationship will be polymorphic. That is, purchasedProducts can contain course records and book records.

As we learned in Chapter 1 – Ember Data Overview, an error will be thrown if we access the purchasedProducts relationship and the related records aren't loaded into the store because the relationship has been declared as synchronous. In the example application, we have the following endpoint to load the related course and book records into the store:

mirage/config.js

```
this.get('/products', function () {
  return {
    courses: [
      {
        id: '5',
        title: 'Introduction to Ember Octane',
        length: '2 hours'
      }
    ],
    books: [
      {
        id: '10',
        title: 'Ember Data in the Wild',
        pages: 100
      }
    ]
  };
});
```

We could also return these resources under a single products key when using the RESTSerializer:

mirage/config.js

```
this.get('/products', function () {
  return {
    products: [
      {
```

```
    id: '5',
    type: 'course',
    title: 'Introduction to Ember Octane',
    length: '2 hours'
  },
  {
    id: '10',
    type: 'book',
    title: 'Ember Data in the Wild',
    pages: 100
  }
 ]
};
});
```

The only requirement here is that we need to include a type property in each product resource, which corresponds to the model name of a "product" subclass.

Polymorphic "belongsTo" Relationships

Now let's see how we can implement the polymorphic belongsTo relationship in Example 2. We'll start by defining content, post, and video models:

app/models/content.js

```
import Model, { attr, hasMany } from '@ember-data/model';

export default class ContentModel extends Model {
  @attr('string') title;
  @hasMany('comment', { async: false }) comments;
}
```

app/models/post.js

```
export default class PostModel extends ContentModel {
  @attr('number') wordCount;
}
```

app/models/video.js

```
import { attr } from '@ember-data/model';
import ContentModel from './content';

export default class VideoModel extends ContentModel {
  @attr('number') length;
}
```

Our post and video models will extend from a base content model which contains the comments relationship.

A comment will belong to a single piece of content, which can be either a post or a video. We can implement this relationship as a polymorphic belongsTo relationship as follows:

app/models/comment.js

```
import Model, { attr, belongsTo } from '@ember-data/model';

export default class CommentModel extends Model {
  @attr('string') body;
  @belongsTo('content', {
    polymorphic: true,
    async: false
  })
  content;
}
```

The content relationship is a standard belongsTo relationship but with a polymorphic option. This will allow us to assign different types of content records to the content relationship as long as those records inherit from the content model.

Next, let's look at the expected response payload for an endpoint that returns all of a user's comments:

mirage/config.js

```
this.get('/comments', function () {
  return {
    comments: [
      {
        id: '1',
        body: 'Looking forward to using all the new features!',
        content: {
          id: '1',
          type: 'post'
        }
      },
      {
        id: '2',
        body: 'Great video! Please make more!',
        content: {
          id: '2',
          type: 'video'
        }
      }
    ],
    posts: [
      {
        id: '1',
        title: 'Ember Octane Released',
        wordCount: 300,
        comments: ['1']
      }
    ],
```

```
    videos: [
      {
        id: '2',
        title: 'Introduction to Ember.js',
        length: 300,
        comments: ['2']
      }
    ]
  };
});
```

Notice how each resource under comments contains a JSON:API Resource Identifier Object under the content property. Similar to the polymorphic hasMany relationship, the id and type will be used to establish a belongsTo relationship with the correct content subclass record.

Customizing Polymorphic Relationship Serialization

In the last two sections, we learned how to define our models and the expected response formats so that hasMany and belongsTo polymorphic relationships get wired up correctly. Now we will look at how to customize a serializer for when an API doesn't follow the default conventions for polymorphic relationships.

In the sample application, head over to http://localhost:4200/ recent-comments and add a comment to one of the items. If you open up the browser console, you will see a request payload with a similar structure to the following:

```
{
  "comment": {
    "body": "My new comment",
    "content": "1",
    "contentType": "post"
  }
}
```

This serialized payload is similar to what we'd expect when serializing any belongsTo relationship, except there is a new key, contentType. The default behavior of the RESTSerializer when serializing polymorphic belongsTo relationships is to create a key where "Type" is appended to the name of the polymorphic relationship. In this case, our polymorphic relationship is named content so the new key becomes contentType.

Let's say we wanted the polymorphic key to be type instead of following the pattern "***Type". We could override the keyForPolymorphicType() method in a serializer:

app/serializers/application.js

```
export default class ApplicationSerializer extends
RESTSerializer {
  keyForPolymorphicType(key, typeClass, method) {
    return 'type';
  }
}
```

Now the request payload will look like the following:

```
{
  "comment": {
    "body": "My new comment",
    "content": "1",
    "type": "post"
  }
}
```

Maybe we would like the request payload to include a JSON:API Resource Identifier Object instead so that there is symmetry between request and response payloads, for example:

```
{
  "comment": {
    "body": "My new comment",
    "content": {
      "id": "1",
      "type": "post"
    }
  }
}
```

We can achieve this by overriding the `serializePolymorphicType()` method:

app/serializers/application.js

```
export default class ApplicationSerializer extends
RESTSerializer {
  serializePolymorphicType(snapshot, json, relationship) {
    super.serializePolymorphicType(snapshot, json,
    relationship);

    let { name } = relationship.meta;

    json[name] = {
      id: json[name],
      type: json[`${name}Type`]
    };

    delete json[`${name}Type`];
  }
}
```

In the preceding code, we are calling `super.serializePolymorphic Type()` to perform the default serialization behavior. This will result in the `json` variable containing an object with a similar structure to the following:

```
{
  comment: {
    body: 'My new comment',
    content: '1',
    contentType: 'post'
  }
}
```

Then, we override the `comment.content` property to be `{ id: '1', type: 'post' }` and delete the `comment.contentType` property.

As we learned in previous chapters, we could also add this logic to a serializer's `serialize()` method, but using the `keyForPolymorphicType()` and `serializePolymorphicType()` methods will likely reduce the amount of code needed for polymorphic relationship serialization.

Customizing Polymorphic Relationship Normalization

Imagine the API serialized the polymorphic `content` relationship in each `comment` resource in the form `type:id`. If this were the case in our sample application, `GET /comments` would return the following JSON:

```
{
  "comments": [
    {
      "id": "1",
      "body": "Looking forward to using all the new features!",
      "content": "post:1"
    },
```

```
    {
      "id": "2",
      "body": "Great video! Please make more!",
      "content": "video:2"
    }
  ],
  "posts": [
    {
      "id": "1",
      "title": "Ember Octane Released",
      "comments": ["1"]
    }
  ],
  "videos": [
    {
      "id": "2",
      "title": "Introduction to Ember.js",
      "comments": ["2"]
    }
  ]
}
```

I know this example is a bit contrived, but you never know what kinds of APIs you'll see in the wild! Before, content contained a JSON:API Resource Identifier Object such as { "id": "1", "type": "post" }. How can we normalize our polymorphic content relationship? We can override one of the many normalization methods that we covered in previous chapters, or we can override the extractPolymorphicRelationship() method. This method gets called for relationships declared with the polymorphic: true option and returns a JSON:API Resource Identifier Object.

Let's assume our polymorphic relationships follow this custom convention and the standard convention. We can override extractPolymorphicRelationship() in our application serializer to account for both scenarios:

app/serializers/application.js

```
export default class ApplicationSerializer extends
RESTSerializer {
  extractPolymorphicRelationship(
    relationshipType,
    relationshipHash,
    relationshipOptions
  ) {
    if (typeof relationshipHash === 'string') {
      let [type, id] = relationshipHash.split(':');
      return { id, type };
    }

    return super.extractPolymorphicRelationship(...arguments);
  }
}
```

In the implementation earlier, relationshipHash will contain post:1 and video:2 for the preceding response. We can split on the colon and create a new object that matches the structure of a JSON:API Resource Identifier Object and return that in the scenario where our custom polymorphic relationship convention is used. Otherwise, we will let the default polymorphic extraction behavior run via super. extractPolymorphicRelationship(...arguments).

Summary

Polymorphism is a powerful concept that allows us to have models that relate to each other through inheritance, and Ember Data relationships can support this. This ultimately allows a `belongsTo` relationship to contain records of different types through a single relationship as long as those records inherit from a common base class. This also allows for a `hasMany` relationship to contain records of multiple types as long as those records inherit from a common base class.

In this chapter, we looked at how to set up our models and API to support polymorphic relationships. We then looked at how we can customize serialization and normalization of polymorphic relationships if our API doesn't follow the default conventions that Ember Data expects. Even though we looked at the implementation of polymorphic relationships with the `RESTSerializer`, the model definitions are the same if you are using one of the other built-in serializers. Additionally, the serializer methods that we overrode are the same, except the `JSONSerializer` and `JSONAPISerializer` don't support the `keyForPolymorphicType()` method. There are also some slight differences in the default API conventions for the `JSONSerializer` and the `JSONAPISerializer`. Despite these minor differences, the patterns and techniques covered in this chapter should equip you to handle polymorphic relationships regardless of which serializer your application is using.

Well, this is the end. Thanks for reading my book! Hopefully, this has helped you and has put you in a good position to work with Ember Data and any custom API. If you have any questions, please reach out to me on Twitter @iamdtang or by email at david@thejsguy.com. I would love to hear about your experiences with Ember Data. You can also stay up to date with my Ember adventures on my blog at `https://davidtang.io`.

Index

U

V, W, X, Y, Z

Printed in the United States
By Bookmasters